Matthew D. Wyatt

An Architect's Note-Book in Spain

Principally illustrating the domestic architecture of that country

Matthew D. Wyatt

An Architect's Note-Book in Spain
Principally illustrating the domestic architecture of that country

ISBN/EAN: 9783337245696

Printed in Europe, USA, Canada, Australia, Japan

Cover: Foto ©Thomas Meinert / pixelio.de

More available books at **www.hansebooks.com**

AN

ARCHITECT'S NOTE-BOOK

IN

SPAIN

PRINCIPALLY ILLUSTRATING THE

DOMESTIC ARCHITECTURE OF THAT COUNTRY.

BY

M. DIGBY WYATT, M.A.

SLADE PROFESSOR OF FINE ART IN THE UNIVERSITY OF CAMBRIDGE, &c.

WITH ONE HUNDRED OF THE AUTHOR'S SKETCHES,

REPRODUCED BY THE AUTOTYPE MECHANICAL PROCESS.

LONDON:

AUTOTYPE FINE ART COMPANY (LIMITED),

36, RATHBONE PLACE.

TO

OWEN JONES, ESQ.

KNIGHT OF THE ORDERS OF SAINTS MAURICE AND LAZARUS OF ITALY, AND OF LEOPOLD OF
BELGIUM, MEMBER OF THE ROYAL ACADEMY OF SAINT FERDINAND OF SPAIN, &c., &c., &c.

—·o——

My dear Owen,

The last book I wrote I dedicated to my brother by blood; the present I dedicate to you— my brother in Art. Let it be a record of the value I set upon all you have taught me, and upon your true friendship.

Ever yours,

M. DIGBY WYATT.

37, Tavistock Place, W.C.
October, 1872.

PREFACE.

EFORE quitting England for a first visit to Spain in the Autumn of 1869, I made up my mind both to see and draw as much of the Architectural remains of that country as the time and means at my disposal would permit; and further determined so to draw as to admit of the publication of my sketches and portions of my notes on the objects represented, in the precise form in which they might be made. I was influenced in this determination by the consciousness that almost from day to day the glorious past was being trampled out in Spain; and that whatever issue, prosperous or otherwise, the fortunes of that much distracted country might take in the future, the minor monuments of Art at least which adorned its soil, would rapidly disappear. Their disappearance would result naturally from what is called "progress" if Spain should revive; while their perishing through neglect and wilful damage, or peculation, would inevitably follow, if the ever smouldering embers of domestic revolution should burst afresh into flame. Such has been the invariable action of those fires which in all history have melted away the most refined evidences of man's intelligence, leaving behind only scanty, and often all but shapeless, relics of the richest and ripest genius.

It is difficult to realise the rapidity with which, almost under one's eyes, the Spain of history and romance "is casting its skin." Travelling even with so recent and so excellent a handbook as O'Shea's of 1869, I noted the following wanton acts of Vandalism and destruction, committed upon monuments of the greatest archæological and artistic interest since he wrote. At Seville, the Church of San Miguel, one of the oldest and finest in the city, was senselessly demolished by the populace as a sort of auto-da-fé, and by way of commemoration of the revolution of September, 1867. In exactly the same way the fine Byzantine churches of San Juan at Lerida, and of San Miguel at Barcelona, have been "improved off the face of the earth." Church plate, Custodias and Virils of the D'Arfés, Becerrias, and other Art workmen, have vanished from the treasuries of all the great ecclesiastical structures, whether sold, melted down, or only hidden, "quien sabe?" The beautiful Moorish decorations of the Alcazar at Segovia had been all but entirely destroyed by fire, attributed to the careless cigar-lighting of the Cadets to whom the structure had been abandoned. The finest old mansion in Barcelona, the Casa de Gralla probably the masterpiece of Damian Forment, and dating from the commencement of the fourteenth century, has been pulled down by the Duke of Medina Celi to form a new street. The beautiful wooden ceiling of the Casa del Infantado at Guadalaxara, the finest of its kind in Spain, in the absence of its owner, who I was told lives in Russia, is coming down in large pieces, and once fallen, I scarcely think it will be in the power of living workmen to make it good again. The exquisite Moorish Palace of the Generalife at Granada, second only to the Alhambra and the Alcazar at Seville, is never visited by its proprietor, and is now one mass of white-wash, a victim of the zeal for cleanliness of a Sanitary "Administrador." In short to visit a Spanish city now, by the light shed upon its ancient glories by the industrious Ponz, is simply to have forced upon one's attention the most striking evidence of the "vanity of human things," and man's inherent tendency to destroy.

One of the most painful sensations the lover of the Art of the Past cannot but experience in Spain, is the feeling of its dissonance from, and irreconcileability with, the wants and economical necessities of to day. The truth is that at the present moment, amongst the many difficult problems which surround and beset the ruling powers, one of the most puzzling is to find fitting uses for the many vast structures which have fallen into the hands of the Government. Churches in number and size out of all proportion to the wants of the population, monasteries entirely without monks, convents with scarcely any nuns, Jesuit seminaries without Jesuits, exchanges without merchants, colleges without students, tribunals of the Holy Inquisition with, thank God! no Inquisitors, and palaces without princes, are really "drugs in the market;" too beautiful to destroy, too costly to properly maintain, and for the original purposes for which they were planned and constructed at incredible outlay they stand now almost useless. For the most part, the grand architectural monuments of the country ~~and~~ are now like Dickens'. "used-up giants" kept only "to wait upon the dwarfs." Among a few instances of such may be noticed, the magnificent foundation of the noblest Spanish ecclesiastic Ximenez. His College at Alca'n de Henares is turned into a young ladies' boarding-school; the splendid Convent of the Knights of Santiago at Leon, the masterpiece of Juan de Badajoz, dedicated to Saint Mark, and one of the finest buildings in

Spain, is now in charge of a solitary policeman and his wife, awaiting its possible conversion into an agricultural college ; the grand Palace of the Dukes of Alva at Seville is let out in numerous small tenements and enriched with unlimited whitewash ; the Colegiata of San Gregorio at Valladolid, another of the magnificent foundations of Cardinal Ximenez, and the old cathedral at Lerida, the richest Byzantine monument in Spain, are now both barracks ;—the vast exchanges of Seville and Zaragoza are tenantless and generally shut up ; the beautiful "Casa de los Abades" at Seville is converted into a boy's school and lodging-house for numerous poor tenants, the Casa del Infante at Zaragoza, containing the most richly sculptured Renaissance Patio in Spain, is chiefly occupied as a livery stable-keeper's establishment ; Cardinal Mendoza's famous Hospital of the Holy Cross at Toledo is now an Infantry College; the great monastery of the Cartuja near Seville, with one of the finest Mudejar wooden ceilings in the country, is turned into Pickman's china factory; the "Taller del Moro" a model Moorish house with its beautiful decorations, at Toledo, is now only a carpenter's workshop and storehouse ; the celebrated establishment of El Cristo de la Victoria at Malaga, with all its glorious associations with the "Reyes Cattolicos," is occupied as a military hospital ; and so on 'ad infinitum.'

Every record the pen and pencil of any accurate observer can preserve at this juncture of the fading glories of the past in Spain is, as it were, snatching a brand from the inevitable fire which has already consumed inestimable treasures upon its soil. It was to give a stamp of truth and authenticity to the few such records I might be enabled to make, that I determined to complete them in the actual presence as it were of the object illustrated, and to admit of no intervention between my own hand, and the eye of any student willing to honour my work with his attention. My sketches might no doubt have gained in beauty by being transcribed on stone or wood by some artist more skilful than I am, but as any such alteration would detract from their simple veracity, I preferred to make them at once upon the spot with anastatic ink, in order that they might be printed just as they were executed. Working with such ink in the open air is difficult, and the result capricious, I have therefore to ask for some indulgence, and to express a hope that any shortcomings in the drawings may be overlooked in the obvious interest of the subjects pourtrayed. Could I but have known, on leaving England, that my sketches could have been so successfully transferred to collodion, and printed therefrom as they have been since my return, I might have spared myself much extra trouble and anxiety, and have probably attained a much better result with less effort.

I have further to ask corresponding indulgence for any literary insufficiencies my text may present. Although for some years a not inattentive student of Spanish art and literature, I could not, and cannot but feel that my acquaintance with the country was and is insufficient for writing worthy notes even upon its architectural monuments, after the excellent works which have been already written by such of my countrymen as Ford, Street, Stirling, and O'Shea. At the same time, considering that to publish my sketches altogether without explanatory letter-press would greatly detract from their interest and consequent usefulness, I have brought into their present shape the scanty notes made upon the spot, more or less directly illustrative of the subject supon which my pencil found occupation.

It will be obvious, it is hoped, that in the selection of subjects for illustration, an endeavour has been made to avoid in any wise trenching upon or clashing with those already fully treated in the admirable work on Spanish Ecclesiastical Architecture by Mr. G. E. Street. Whilst he has turned from, I have turned towards, the Plateresque and later styles of Spain, and whilst he has apparently sought specially for what might be useful to church-builders, my aim has been rather to collect hints for house-builders. Thanks to him, and others like him, we have now been left probably with more to learn in the latter direction than in the former.

The following was my line of tour, and as it comprises most of what is, I believe, best worth seeing in Spain in the way of Art, with the notable exceptions of Santiago, Oviedo, Murcia, Cuenca, Placencia, Alicante and Valencia, which want of time did not permit me to include, I do not hesitate to commend it to those, desirous, as I was, of seeing as much as possible of what was excellent or curious within a short space of time. It was as follows, from London viâ Paris, Bordeaux, and Bayonne to Spain, beginning with Burgos, then successively visiting Valladolid (rail), Venta de Baños (rail), Leon (rail), Zamora and Salamanca, (by "diligence" from Leon) Avila (by "diligence" from Salamanca) Escorial (rail), Madrid (rail), Segovia (by "diligence" from Madrid and back), Alcala de Heñares (by rail from Madrid and back), Toledo (by rail from Madrid and back), Cordoba (rail), Sevilla (rail), Cadiz (by the Guadalquivir steamer), Gibraltar (by steamer), Malaga (by steamer), Granada (rail and "diligence,") Andujar ("diligence,") Madrid (rail), a second time, Guadalajara (rail), Zaragoza (rail), Lerida (rail), Barcelona (rail), and Gerona (rail), thence to the frontier by "diligence," and home by rail, viâ Perpignan, Carcassonne, Toulouse and Paris.

To preserve some sort of order, I have arranged my sketches as they were executed in point of time, and thrown my notes into a corresponding sequence.

To assert that Spain can teach the lessons to the architect which may be gained from Italy, or even from France would, I think, be to claim too much for her, but on the other hand, it should be remembered, that it is a mine which has been very much less exhausted. To the interest and grandeur of its Northern Gothic buildings, Mr. Street has done a justice long denied to them; while Girault de Prangey, and above all Owen Jones, have helped us to a right appreciation of the works of those masterly artificers, the Moors, who seem to have possessed an intuitive love for the beautiful in structure.

It is with no small pleasure that I have laboured to direct attention to other monuments, than those they have so satisfactorily illustrated, of a land from travelling in which I have derived great delight, and much instruction.

If asked what predominant sensation Spanish Architecture had produced in my mind, I think I should be inclined to say, that of the manifestation of an entire indifference to expense. No one appears to have counted the cost of the work upon which he engaged. Whether it was a mediæval architect entering upon the vast construction of Cathedrals, such as Seville, Toledo or Leon, a Renaissance architect dashing upon the immense laying out of buildings such as the Cathedrals of Salamanca or Granada, or an Herrera plunging into such stone quarries as the Escorial or the Cathedral at Valladolid, not a shadow of doubt ever seems to have crossed the mind of the beginners, that some one—never mind who—would complete what they began.

Such peculiarities of national character are apt to beget proverbs, and

we accordingly find the grave ponderosity, and at the same time, power
of the Spaniard in the undertakings of his palmy days, thus characterised
in comparison with those of the other peoples of Europe.

"In their undertakings," says "Der curieuse Antiquarius durch
Europam,"[*] the natives of different European countries are said by old
legends to proceed thus :—

> "Der Frantzose wie ein Adler,
> Der Deutsche wie ein Bär,
> Der Italianer wie ein Fuchs,
> Der Spanier wie ein Elephant,
> Der Engeländer wie ein Löw."[†]

To some, and but few, Spanish architects was it given to see ended
what they commenced, and even such favourites of fortune generally
suffered from a curtailment of their too ambitious designs.

I could not but feel, in looking at the works of Herrera, and indeed at
those of several other men, such as Diego de Siloe, Gil de Ontañon,
Henrique de Egas, Alonso Covarrubbias, and Juan de Badajoz, that there
exists for architecture a just mean between their frequent extravagance,
and the sordid andshab by spirit in which we from time to time approach
the question of expenditure upon "public works." The economy which
consists in sobriety and simplicity of parts, especially in structures
destined to subserve ordinary uses, is as much to be admired, as the
economy which aims at the combination of magnificence with "cheese-
paring" is to be deprecated and despised.

[*] Von P. L. Berckenmeyern. Hamburg, 1731.

[†] "The Frenchman like an eagle. The German like a bear. The Italian like a fox. The
Spaniard like an Elephant. The Englishman like a lion."

CONTENTS.

·BVRGOS·
·THE·ARCO·DE·SANTA·MARIA·

PLATE I.

BURGOS.

THE ARCO DE SANTA MARIA.

I T is sad to notice how few traces beyond its magnificent
Cathedral are left in this, the capital of old Castile, of those
"Castellanos rancios y viejos," who once so splendidly represented the
pride and power of Spanish chivalry. Of the sixteen golden castles
the city bears upon its stately arms how insignificant are the relics?
The remains of its walls and bastions attest the many centuries
during which it held its own against all comers, Christian or
Infidel. Of these walls, our sketch represents a portion in which
there is little doubt the Renaissance frontispiece and archway replaced
an older and sterner portal, better suited probably for defence than
decoration. The legend runs that this façade was executed by the
citizens, who had been exhibiting proclivities of far too Communistic
a character to be agreeable to so high-handed a sovereign as
Charles V., in order to propitiate that potentate, and to commemorate
a visit, on his part at least, of a conciliatory character. It would
seem, however, that in spite of the loyalty which induced the
Burgalese to assign the post of honour (always under the invocation
of their crowning tutelary the "Virgen sin pecado concebida)" to

the statue of the King, they took good care to give him for companions Nuño Rasura, and Lain Calvo, whom they had themselves elected in the tenth century to rule over them, and protect their Communal rights. The maintenance of these had been somewhat interfered with by the King of Leon, Fruela II., who had invited the chief citizens to a banquet, and then quietly removed them out of his royal way by summarily putting them all to death. Amongst other statues which adorn this gateway are to be found those of Don Diego Parcelos, the founder of the city in 884, of the Cid—the pride of Spain and especially of Burgos, in which city he was born, and where his bones still rest—and of Fernan Gonzalez who redeemed the district from the yoke of the Kings of Leon, to whom it had been tributary, and who constituted himself and his family ~~as~~ its protectors, under the style and title of Condes de Castilla.

The architecture of this frontispiece which gains great importance and much picturesque effect from its association with the bartizans and turrets of the mediæval gateway, has been attributed to Felipe de Borgoña, not apparently on any other grounds than the facts that he was ~~a native~~ of the city in whom his fellow-citizens felt great pride, and that he was employed upon the "Crucero" of the cathedral at about the period when this grand portal was probably erected.

— an inhabitant

BVRGOS · LCASA DE MIRANDA

PLATE II.

~~

BURGOS.

PATIO OF THE CASA DE MIRANDA.

THIS plate introduces us ~~at once~~ to the most striking feature of all important Spanish houses, the Patio, or internal courtyard, answering to and perpetuating the Atrium of Roman architecture, with its impluvium and compluvium, and corresponding with the ordinary Cortile of the Italians. It is usually rectangular in plan, and ~~is~~ entirely surrounded upon at least two stories by arcading behind which run passages into which open the doors of every principal set of apartments of the house. There are rarely many windows in the walls of the Patios, as the rooms generally occupy the whole width intervening between the Patio walls, and the external walls of the house from which the light is mainly derived. There are, however, usually more windows on the lower story of the Patio than on the upper, since the chief saloons requiring most light were on the first floor, while much of the lower floor was occupied as was also usual in Italy, by retainers, servants, poor guests, ~~stewards~~ and administradores—to say nothing of mules, and horses with stores and munitions of all sorts.

Mendicant friars/

Nothing can be more picturesque or better suited to the climate than these Patios, since owing to the deep arcades which surround the open part (the ~~Templavium~~) of the court-yard upon more stories than one, there is always some portion of the arcade in which shelter can be obtained from sun, rain, or wind, and in which the occupants of the several apartments can sit and work, or lounge and smoke, in abundant but not unbearable light, and perfect comfort. This facility of outlet enables them, during the hours when the sun shines most fiercely, to keep their living and sleeping rooms dark and cool, and in exactly the state to make the midday meal and subsequent siesta truly luxurious and refreshing.

One open staircase usually connects the upper and lower arcades; admission is rarely given to the whole building at more than one point, the great door, adjoining which is almost always to be found the concierge, the janitor of the old Roman house, upon the model of which the Spaniards probably founded their notion of a residence at once noble and comfortable.

Little need be said concerning the particular house sketched. It is one of the few left in Burgos to bear witness to the grandeur of its old aristocracy. Though once the residence of the powerful Condes de Miranda of the family of the Zunigas, it is now but a half ruined and entirely dirty lodging-house for the lower classes in a poor and neglected part of the city. A fine dedication to the most illustrious "Señor Don Francisco de çuñiga y Avellaneda, Conde de Miranda Señor de la Villa Daça, y de la Casa de Avellaneda by Pedro Martinez the Printer of Seville, in 1565 sets forth the arms as well as the style and title of the nobleman by whom, or by whose next descendant the "Casa de Miranda" of Burgos was probably built.

The present representative of this family is no other than the Conde de Montijo, head of the house to which Her Majesty the Empress of the French belongs. The remarkable "Casa solar" of Peñaranda de Duero, within an easy excursion from Burgos, once a magnificent villa of the Zunigas, was one of the hereditary possessions of her sister the Duchess of Alba.

There are some few other old houses remaining in Burgos, the most remarkable, for oddity rather than beauty, being the "Casa del Cordon;" so called from its façade, which exhibits a gigantic rope representing the "Cordon" of the Teutonic order, encircling and uniting, the arms of the Velascos, Mendozas, and Figueras with those of Royalty. It was erected by a Count Haro, Constable of Castile at the end of the fifteenth century. It is now the residence of the Capitan General of the Province, and the property of the Duca de Frias, a descendant of Count Haro.

The Casa de Miranda is to be found in Burgos, in the "Calle de la Calera," not far from the "Barrio de la Vega." No English visitor to Burgos should omit to see the Convent of las Huelgas, most interesting not only as founded by an English Princess, (Leonora, daughter of Henry II, married to Alfonso VIII), in 1180; but as evidencing in its design, which is exceptionally grave, simple, and well proportioned, an unquestionable English architectural influence.

Of the Cathedral, remains of the Castle, and the Convent of the Cartuja it is needless to speak here, since they are certain not to be overlooked by the traveller. Mr. Waring, who has so well drawn

the marvels of the last mentioned building,* has given some pretty
illustrations of ornamental detail from the fine Renaissance "Ospedal
del Rey," which may be found not far from the Convent of las
Huelgas.*

* Waring (John Burley) Architectural, Sculptural, and Picturesque Studies of Burgos
and its neighbourhood. Folio. London. 1852.

† Examples of Architectural Art in Italy and Spain. Folio. London. 1850.

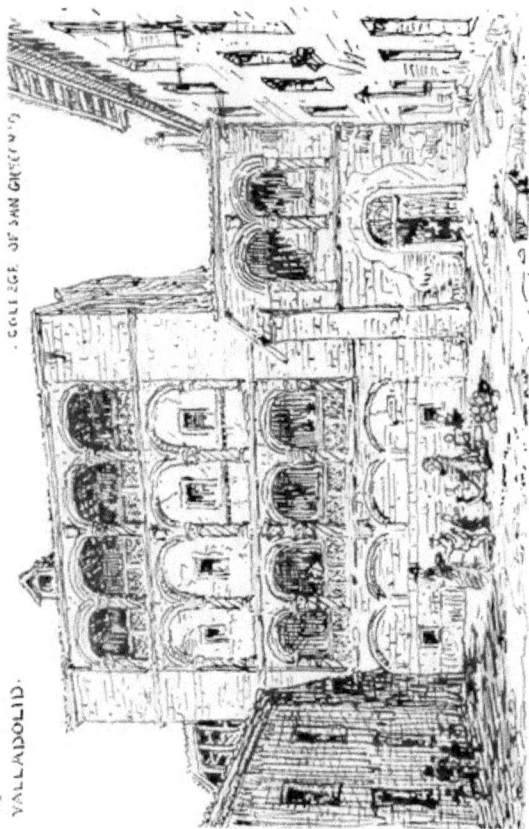

VALLADOLID. . COLLEGE OF SAN GREGORIO.

PLATE III.

VALLADOLID.

COLEGIO DE SAN GREGORIO.

FROM early in the fifteenth century, through the reigns of Juan II. and his successors, until the elevation of Madrid into the Capital by Charles the Fifth, and into the only and official seat of the Court by Philip II. Valladolid was emphatically the Royal city of Spain. It is there, accordingly, that the traveller would naturally look for relics of Royal and courtly magnificence as displayed in the stirring times during which the over-elaboration of Gothic Art began to merge itself, in sympathy with the Medicean energies of Rome and Florence, into the style of the Renaissance as practised at a later date by many citizens of Valladolid, such as Antonio de Arphe, and Juan de Arphe y Villafañe, master-workers in gold and silver; as Juan de Juni, and Hernandez, the marvellous wood-carvers and sculptors, authors of the peculiar gilt painted groups for which the city became so famous; and as Alonzo Berruguete, Henrique de Egas, and Macias Carpintero "masters of works" of no mean repute. Of all the glorious works these men and their disciples and contemporaries produced in Valladolid a few "disjecta membra" alone remain. Of the very building, an outlying fragment of which forms the subject of the sketch under notice, all but the actual structure was destroyed by the French under Napoleon I. in person, who in 1809 inaugurated a reign of terror in the city. "No where," in Spain, as Ford writes in 1845, "has recent destruction been more busy (than in Valladolid) ; witness San Benito, San Diego, San Francisco, San Gabriel, &c., almost swept away, their precious altars broken, their splendid sepulchres dashed to pieces ; hence the sad void created in the treasures of art and religion which are recorded by previous travellers while now-a-days the native in this mania of modernising is fast destroying those venerable vestiges of Charles V. and Philip II. which escaped the Gaul." The situation of this city on the direct line of railway communication between France and Madrid has greatly helped forward this "modernising" and even as this is written, numerous old streets are being pulled down to make way for the convenient, but far from picturesque monotony in which the nineteenth century usually writes its date upon its street architecture. In one respect, especially, the glory of Valladolid has entirely departed. In this, the city of the Arphes, in which as Navagiero* says, (writing in 1525, "Sono in Valladolid assai artefeci di ogni sorte, é se vi lavora benissimo de tutte le arti, e sopra tutto d'argenti, e vi sono tanti argenteri quanti non sono in due altre terre," no gold or silversmith's work is to be found worthy a moment's attention. The "Plateria" still remains, and the shops of the Plateros still abound, but, with the exception of two or three little old fragments saved from the melting pot, the elegant types of the "Varia commensuracion" of Villafañe have disappeared, giving place to poor imitations of bad French work.

* "Viaggio in Spagna," quoted by O'Shea, page 498.

VALLADOLID
PATIO DI SAN
GREGORIO.

PLATE IV

VALLADOLID.

DETAIL FROM THE "PATIO DE SAN GREGORIO."

THE portion of the great Dominican Convent of Valladolid which formed the subject of the last sketch, is supposed to have been the commencement of a second Patio, or courtyard, around which were to have been arranged apartments, mainly intended for the reception of guests or visitors, lay as well as ecclesiastic. The arcading, of which Plate IV is a sketch, surrounds the great Patio of the monastic establishment of which the "Colegio" proper is the Church. Around this noble courtyard were grouped the apartments in which resided the powerful Black Friars—so called from their dress— worthy adherents to the traditions of the founder of the Order, himself an old Castilian, whose activity as Preachers, and still more as Inquisitors, made them, perhaps, even more powerful in controlling the destinies of the Peninsula than the political heads of the State. The first stone of this great establishment, dedicated to St. Gregory, and founded by Alonso of Burgos, Bishop of Palencia, was laid in the year 1488. Some idea of the rapid growth and elevation of the Dominicans about this period may be derived from an observation of the fact that this splendid Church and Monastery was the second great establishment of the Order in Valladolid completed within the space of about ten years. Cean Bermudez tells us that the Cardinal Don Juan Torquemada caused the Church of the Convent of St. Paul to be erected, which, with its façade of excellent architecture, was finished in the year 1463.

The work at Saint Gregory lasted about eight years, a very short time, considering not only the quantity and extent of labour involved in the mere construction, but the amount of intricate and elaborate sculpture which decorates the façade of the Church. Its architect, Macias Carpentero, of Medino del Campo, is placed by Llaguno y Amirola upon a footing, as to merit, with the celebrated architects Siloe and Cruz of Cologne, who introduced extraordinary elaboration into the ornamental carving of Spain. The fate of Macias was a sad one, since on the last Saturday in July, in the year 1490, while working himself, and directing this great architectural work, he committed suicide, infinitely to the surprise and regret of the monks and their fellow-citizens.

Some idea of the scale upon which the Patio of San Gregorio is worked out, may be derived from a knowledge of the facts, that the lower arcade is about twenty feet high, and the upper fifteen feet. The open space enclosed by the arcading is very large, and the distance from centre to centre of each of the pillars about nine feet.

VALLADOLID.

PATIO DE SAN GREGORIO.

PLATE V.

VALLADOLID.

SMALL PATIO DE SAN GREGORIO.

IN that material—stucco—which we of the nineteenth century affect to despise, and in the use of which both the Romans and the Great Masters of the Renaissance, under Raffaelle's guidance, excelled, the Moors delighted. By its use they were able, with speed and accuracy, to supply the redundancy of conventional ornament essential to contrast with the rigid geometrical setting out of lines and compartments which formed a fundamental law of their beautiful style of design. Their aptitude in the manipulation of this material did not desert them when their talents were called into operation by their Christian Masters. Of this the pretty window which forms the chief feature of the sketch under consideration, offers an agreeable proof. At the first glance, one might have fancied that this window was of earlier date than the gothic stone arch beneath, and indeed a relic of the Moorish occupation of Valladolid before the Christians reconquered the district, so different in style are its details from those of the arch. To have encountered the difficulties of constructing such an arch beneath, without destroying such a window, is, however, so contrary to all ancient precedents in similar cases, that any such theory must be dismissed on reflexion, and an explanation sought in some other direction. It is to be found in the fact, that about the middle of the fifteenth century, shortly after which date, both arch and window were probably constructed, the Christians had plenty of skilful artificers in stone, who possessed no aptitude for working in stucco, whilst the Moors executed but little ornament in stone, but much in brick and plaster. Hence the marked difference in style which is apparent between the window sketched, and the architectural detail of the rest of this pretty little court, which is shown on this sketch, and the one which follows it.

The rooms surrounding the Arcade of this Patio, and the Arcade itself, are now used as a " Corps de Garde" in connection with the Government offices of the great Patio of this " Colegio." They naturally, therefore, rejoice in the rapidly accumulating whitewash, which serves very generally in Spain, at once as a panacea against cholera and fever, and the obliterator of all useless excrescences in the nature of Architectural Ornament.

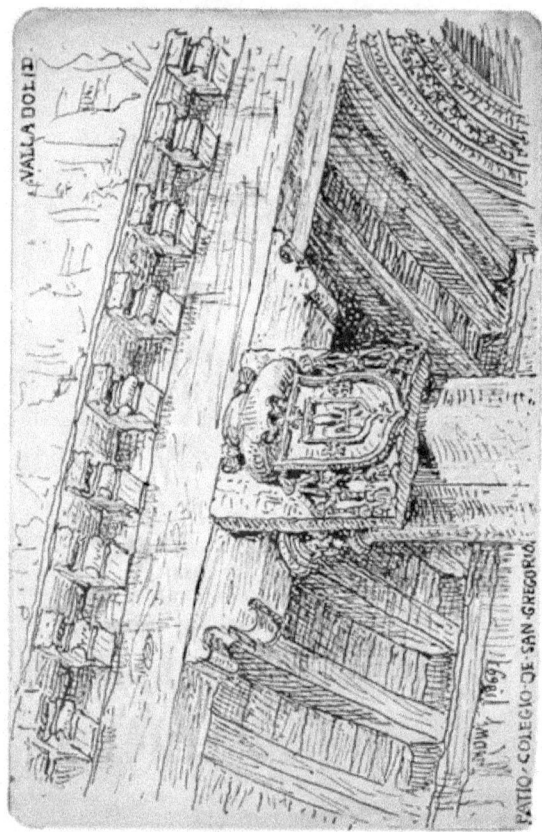

VALLADOLID

PATIO · COLEGIO · DE · SAN · GREGORIO

PLATE VI.

VALLADOLID.

SMALL PATIO, COLEGIO DE SAN GREGORIO.

THE stucco upper-storey from which the last sketch (Plate V) was taken rests upon a lower open storey, forming the usual recessed Arcade or Colonade of even very humble Patios. In this case, the columns, on two sides, (the upper parts of one of which are shown) including the coat-of-arms, are in stone; while the brackets easing the compression of the fibres, and shortening the bearing of the beams, the beams themselves, and the row of brackets above, being really only the moulded ends of the joists of the upper floor, are all in wood. They thus illustrate the combination of materials in construction so much affected by the Moors. At the same time the architectural details shown both in this sketch, and in the one which precedes it, exhibit certain ornamental features derived from Arabian models. That there should be no question in this structure, however, as to the ascendency of the Christian over the Moor, the proud Cardinal has affixed his arms, in which the Church's sacred emblems of the fleur-de-lys and cross forcibly express the favourite tenets of the Spaniard.

Few cities of Spain more rejoiced in heraldic devices than did

Valladolid, the especial seat of the Castilian nobility, at least until its removal to Madrid.   Amongst all the beautiful fac-similes of finely mantled, and well displayed escutcheons which adorn the works of early printers, given to us by Sir Stirling Maxwell, few excel those which issued from the presses of the Valladolid printers.   The Germans who followed in the train, or, at any rate under the auspices, of Charles V., no doubt set the fashion at the commencement of the century at Seville, which was taken up by Spaniards towards the middle of the same century at Valladolid.   Francesco Fernandez de Cordova appears to have been the great master of the craft there, and and splendid are the heraldic frontispieces of his books from 1548 onwards.   His style, at any rate, was maintained in his family till near the end of the century, as the title-page of the celebrated " Quilatador de la Plata oro y piedras," by Joan Arphe, 1572, displays the arms of the Cardinal Bishop of Siguenza, drawn by, and bearing the initials of, no less an artist than Arphe y Villafañe himself.   The imprint of the volume bears no longer the name of Francisco, but the names of Alonzo y Diego Fernandez de Cordova.

The finest specimen of Francisco's work, given by Sir Stirling Maxwell, is the grand heading to a proclamation issued by Charles V, in 1549.   It exhibits not only the Royal and Imperial escutcheon, Double-headed Eagle, and Columns, with the proud motto " plus ultra," but a quantity of pure Renaissance ornament from which all trace of Gothic has disappeared.

* Examples of Ornamental Heraldry of the sixteenth century.   London, 1867.   Privately printed.

VALLADOLID
LA·CASA·DEL·
INFANTADO·

·M·W·1889·

PLATE VII.

VALLADOLID.

LA CASA ~~DE EL~~ INFANTADO.

del

AS in Italy, so in Spain, the architecture of the revival may be
divided into at least two great schools, viz., the early, in
which sculpture, and particularly sculptured arabesque, play a prominent
part; and the late, in which regularity in the use of the orders and
a system of rigidly proportioned plain architectural members form
the main constituents of the most highly commended structures.
Both merged into the extravagance which follows when architects
learn to draw with facility rather than to think with steadfastness
and propriety. As Italy had its Borromini, so had Spain its
Churriguerra.

The building from which my sketch has been taken belongs to
the second of these divisions of the architecture of the revival, as
may be seen by the grave simplicity of the Ionic columns which
support the massive but plain arches of both stories of a large and
pretentious Patio. In this sketch I have chosen the point of view
from the entrance loggia of the house, because looking from it I
could well see, and therefore illustrate, the way in which a grand
staircase, covered at the top, but open to the air upon one side,

usually connects, in large houses, the upper and lower arcades of the Patios, and consequently the upper and lower floors of the mansion which open on to the two main arcades. The staircase is very rarely closed in any way, by iron-work or otherwise; consequently the visitor once obtaining access to the Patio was and is at liberty to ramble nearly all over the house un-checked. As front doors usually stand open from morning till night, access to Patios may generally be freely obtained; but where the house is inhabited by one family only, or by more than one family desiring privacy, iron or wooden doors usually close openings to the Patio such as are shown in the sketch. It is only when in answer to a bell, or knocker, attached to this or to an external doorway, a servant has appeared and ascertained that the visitor is an "amigo," that the door itself is opened, and access to the interior afforded.

It is a popular prejudice that gravity in Spanish architecture only came in with Herrera, after the middle of the fifteenth century in Spain, but in reality there were several other men who before him asserted their dissent from the plateresque redundancy of ornament, and designed works upon a careful study of Italian models of architectural proportion. Among such may be reckoned Pedro Machuca who in 1526 designed the palace of Charles V. at Granada, Alonzo Covarrubias who was architect for the noble staircase and cartile of the Alcazar at Toledo, and Diego Siloe who a few years later created the fine Cathedral of Granada.

·LEON·
·SAN·ISIDRO·

PLATE VIII.

LEON.

CHURCH OF SAN ISIDRO.

THE antiquity of the city of Leon and its importance as a
Roman station are well shown by its picturesque and strong
walls, which in many places yet exhibit clearly Roman masonry
in the substructure and general form. Other places, subsequent
generations of artificers have left unmistakeable autographs inscribed
in most legible and durable forms, attesting dates of construction,
dilapidation, restoration, and then again dilapidation, through centuries
of tempestuous existence. One of the most picturesque bastions of
these old walls is the one shown in my sketch which groups
exceedingly well with the fine Romanesque steeple of San Isidro,
which stands on the west of the Church altogether detached from it.
Both Church and steeple date from about the middle of the twelfth
century, and possess great historical and architectural interest. Their
historical interest is due to their association with the fervidly pious Queen
Sancha; and to the fact that in the Pantheon, or chapel dedicated
to Santa Catilina at the north-west end of the Church, probably
grouped around the body of the Saint, repose Kings and Queens of
Spain from Fernando I. and Doña Sancha the founders of the

Church, through eight generations. Their architectural interest is derivable from the constructional and ornamental details dwelt upon by Mr. Street, to whose excellent account of the building the reader may be referred.

LEON.
SAN·MARCOS·

PLATE IX.

—

LEON.

CONVENT OF SAN MARCOS.

O N the 3rd of September, 1512, a meeting took place between
certain ecclesiastics of the Chapter of Salamanca, and nine of
the most famous architects of Spain, the minute or "procès verbale"
of which would form a model for what might often be done with great
advantage to all concerned in this country in the initiation of any great
architectural work. The object of the Junta was to settle the principal
difficulties of the design of the new Cathedral of Salamanca, then about
to be begun. Interesting as are all the conclusions arrived at upon this
memorable occasion, it is not with them we have now to concern
ourselves, but with the circumstance only that, amongst the signatures
attached to the document[*] occurs that of Juan de Badajoz, the architect
of the noble façade of the celebrated Convent of the Knights of
Santiago at Leon, which forms the subject of our ninth sketch. In the
following year to that of the meeting at Salamanca, Juan de Badajoz
was summoned in concert with Juan Gil de Hontañon and

[*] Given at length under the No. XXXV in the Appendix to the First Volume of the
" Noticias de los Arquitectos y Arquitectura de España, &c.," por Señor D. Eugenio Llaguno
y Amirola, &c. Madrid, 1829.

Juan de Alava to report on the repairs necessary to the Cathedral
at Seville. For this he was paid by the Chapter one hundred
ducats, no mean sum in those days. Called from Seville to Leon,
Badajoz seems to have immediately set in hand the Capilla Mayor
of the Church of San Isidro. In Leon and elsewhere he appears
to have been much employed, until in 1537 he commenced the
Convent of San Zoil at Carrion (about twelve leagues from Leon,)
for the Condes of that place. The taste for elaborate ornamental
sculpture greatly increasing at that time, Juan de Badajoz seems to
have taken pains to surround himself with the most skilful carvers
of his days, and on all occasions to have pushed them forwards as
their merits deserved. Hence, when called upon, shortly after setting
in hand the works at Carrion, to commence the even more elaborate
and important ones of San Marcos, he was able to carry on the two
for a time concurrently, and ultimately to resign the charge of what
he began and advanced considerably single-handed, to his deputy,
Pedro di Castrillo.

On San Marcos Juan de Badajoz appears to have worked
pertinaciously, at any rate until the year 1543, when more than half
the whole work was completed. In the sculpture, of which there is
an enormous quantity, he had the assistance, as principal sculptor, of
Guillermo Doncel. The ornamental details are excellent, far better
than those involving a knowledge of the proportions and forms of
the human figure. The size of the building is enormous, and its
general effect very picturesque. The works appear to have been
suspended while still far from complete. They were not resumed
until the year 1715.

MDW 1883 LEONE SAN MARCO

PLATE X.

. . .

LEON.

CLOISTER OF THE CONVENT OF SAN MARCOS.

brothers of the

IT used to be a proud old boast of the Military Order of
Sant' Iago that their Palace, or Convent, call it which you will,
at Leon, was quite as fine and spacious as the palace occupied by
the Kings of Spain at Madrid. Knowing this, I visited it with a
certain amount of apprehension as to my reception by such
descendants of the magnates of old, as might still occupy the
building. My fears were groundless, for I found after much
knocking and ringing, that a solitary policeman was the only
occasional tenant of its vast halls, and almost numberless rooms.
It was indeed melancholy to see such a structure so evidently and
entirely "out of joint with fortune" and "the times," as to be
apparently inapplicable and inconvertible to any useful purpose.

With the impressions received from meeting with such a state
of things, the traveller naturally feels a difficulty in realising the
fact that the extent and splendour of this Convent actually
represented what was once a vital principle of first importance to
Spain. To her, until Mariolatry set in with full intensity, the name
of Sant' Iago was a tower of strength. Not only did the possession

of the shrine to which pilgrims flocked, even from beyond the seas in thousands, bring wealth to the Church; but the elevation of the Saint into an actual soldier of the Faith, a leader to material as well as to spiritual victory, supplied for Spain that fervour under arms which, when passing under the form of devotion to "the Prophet" had, as both Church and State in Spain wisely recognised, wrought such marvels in the consolidation of the power of her natural enemies, the Moors. By the creation of the religious orders of cavaliers, or rather of the military orders of priests, Spain at once nourished the spirit of chivalry and the Christian Faith, (which ultimately won for her the reconquest of all that Mahommedan Chivalry and Mahommedan Faith had conquered from her.[*] The very length and pertinacity of the struggle only served to quicken the devotion of the people to their "Gran Capitan," Sant' Iago, and to induce them to enrich to the utmost the order which bore his name.

Hence the magnificent scale of buildings, such as the Convent of San Marcos, the stately cloisters of which once sheltered those whose energy in council and skill in the field maintained that life and action for the warlike, and protection and repose for the peaceable, which were essential to the consolidation and upholding of the monarchy of Spain, and its supposed indispensable and inseparable adjunct the "Catholic Faith."

[*] See "Historia de las ordenes Militares de S. Iago," por F. Caro de Torres. Madrid, 1629. Folio.

LEON.
CASA DE LOS GUZMANES.

PLATE XI.

LEON.

EXTERIOR OF THE CASA DE LOS GUSMANES.

IN an ancient house which stood upon the site on which now stands the Palace which forms the subject of our sketch, there was born, in the year 1266, a "Cavalier," who, when arrived at manhood, followed the fortunes of Sancho the Brave. After many struggles, the King having taken Tarifa in Andalucia from the Moors in 1292, looked round amongst his followers for one willing to hold what he had won. All refused, owing to the danger of the position, until Alonzo Perez de Guzman, the Cavalier in question, offered to keep possession of the town for a year. The story is thus condensed by Ford, from the " Romancero." The Moors beleaguered it, aided by the Infante Juan, a traitor brother of Sancho's to whom Alonso's eldest son, aged nine, had been entrusted previously as a page. " Juan now brought the boy under the walls, and threatened to kill him if his father would not surrender the place. Alonso drew his dagger and threw it down exclaiming, ' I prefer honour without a son, to a son with dishonour.' He retired, and the Prince caused the child to be put to death. A cry of horror ran through the Spanish battlements. Alonso rushed forth, beheld his son's body, and returning to his childless mother, calmly observed, 'I feared that the infidel had gained the city.' Sancho, the King, likened him to Abraham, from this parental sacrifice and honoured him with the 'canting' name 'El Bueno.' The good (Guzman, Gutman, Goodman.) He became the founder of the princely Dukes of Medina Sidonia, now merged by marriage in the Villafrancas." From this great head descended ultimately Her Majesty the Empress Eugénie of France. Gaining strength, riches and power, the original residence of El Bueno became too small for his aspiring family, and in 1560, Don Juan Quiñones y Guzman, Bishop of Calahorra, determined upon the erection, on the same site, of the present fine structure. The name of the architect does not seem to be known, but it is obviously the work of one who, rejecting the elaboration of the Plateresque style, followed the simpler and more chastened proportions ~~with which they became acquainted through the works~~ of the early Italian writers on architecture, such as Alberti and Serlio. It is probable that the use of a large quantity of iron externally, as in the balconies of this Palace ~~and elsewhere~~ was somewhat of a novelty at the date of construction, since the story runs "that when Philip II. visited Leon, as his courtiers, some friends of the Bishops, were praising the building, and were mentioning in a friendly way the thousands of cwts. of iron employed in it, the King severely observed, punningly by the way, 'En verdad que ha sido mucho yerro para un obispo."

The pun turns upon the word *yerro* which means both iron, and a mistake. The joke would have been unworthy of Philip II. if it had not been grim.

* O'Shea. Page 236.

PLATE 2

LEON.

CASA DE LOS GUSMANES

PLATE XII.

—

LEON.

PATIO OF THE CASA DE LOS GUSMANES.

dependant.

PALACES, such as supply our twelfth illustration, are now rarely
occupied in Spain by one family only. Instead of serving as
the place of general rendezvous for the relations and intimate friends
only of the aristocratic proprietor, the Patios are now usually peopled
with men, women and children belonging to the numerous families,
between whom the occupation of the Palace, sadly fallen from its
high estate, is divided. Instead of the mansion being guarded by a
grand inquisitor in the shape of a porter, with armed servants within
hail, with almost more than Oriental jealousy, as in the old days, he
who will, may usually find entrance or exit unheeded, passing but
as one more or one less of the hundreds who go to and fro in the
course of the day to the various apartments which are frequently let
and sublet, at ridiculously low rents, to poor occupants who can afford
to pay no other. Poverty, in fact, revels in halls where magnificence
once reigned supreme.

It is no easy task for the imagination to repeople such old
grand residences with the stately Hidalgoes and Señoras, who once
occupied and maintained them with scrupulous care and princely dignity.

Happily, the Countess d'Aulnois comes to our aid with her lively
account of the dwelling at Madrid of the Duchess of Terra Nueva,
appointed Camerera-Mayor to the young Queen, in 1679; and her
picturesque sketch may be freely accepted as expressing the general
style in which families of dignity, such as the Guzmanes, magnates
of Leon, lived during the plenitude of Spanish wealth and power.

"One can hardly see anything," says she,[*] "that looks more
splendid than this house of theirs; they use the upper apartments,
which are hung with tapestry, all done with raised work of gold.
In one great chamber, which is longer than it is broad, you may see
several glass doors, which go into closets, or little cells; the first of
which is the Duchess of Terra Nova's, hung with grey, and a bed of
the same, and all other things very plain. On one side lodges her
daughter, the Duchess of Monteleon, who is a widow, and has her
room furnished like her mother's. Afterwards you come to the Princess
of Monteleon's chamber, which is not larger than the others; but
her bed is of gold and green damask, lined with silver brocade, and
trimmed with Point-de-Spain. The sheets were laced about with an
English lace of half an ell deep. Over against it were the chambers
of Monteleon and Hijar's children, which were furnished with white
damask. Next to these is the little chamber of the Duchess Hijar,
furnished with crimson coloured velvet upon a gold ground. Their
rooms were no otherwise divided than by partitions of a certain sweet
wood; and they told me that six of their women lay in their chambers
upon beds brought thither at night. The ladies were in a great gallery,
spread with a very rich foot-cloth. There were set round it crimson

[*] Ingenious and diverting letters of "A Lady's Travels into Spain," London, 1774, Vol. I. page 218.

coloured velvet cushions embroidered with gold, and they are longer than they are broad. There were also several great cabinets inlaid, and adorned with precious stones; but they are not made in Spain. And between them were tables of silver, and admirable looking-glasses, both for their largeness and rich frames, the worst of which were of silver. But that which I thought finest, were their escaparates, which is a certain sort of close cabinet with one great glass, and filled with all the rarities which one can imagine, whether it be in amber, porcelain, crystal, bezoar-stone, branches of coral, mother-of-pearl, filligreen in gold, and a thousand other things of value."

CALLE
DELLA TESORIERA.

LEON.

PLATE XIII.

LEON.

DETAIL FROM A HOUSE IN THE CALLE DE LA TESORIERA.

THIS pretty little keystone, with its acanthus leaf well drawn and freely cut in good cinque-cento style occurs over the Portal of an old house in one of the secondary streets of Leon. The pot of lilies which surmounts it is a pretty little "impresa," quaintly signifying the devotion of the owner of the house to the especial object of every good Spaniard's worship, the most holy Virgin "sin pecado concebida." The S shaped irons, which appear on the right and left of the pot of lilies, serve to help to support the light balcony, which generally occurs over entrance doors of minor importance in Spain, and which often serves as a small open air addition to the common sitting-room, in which the women of the house do much of the usual needle work, spinning, &c.

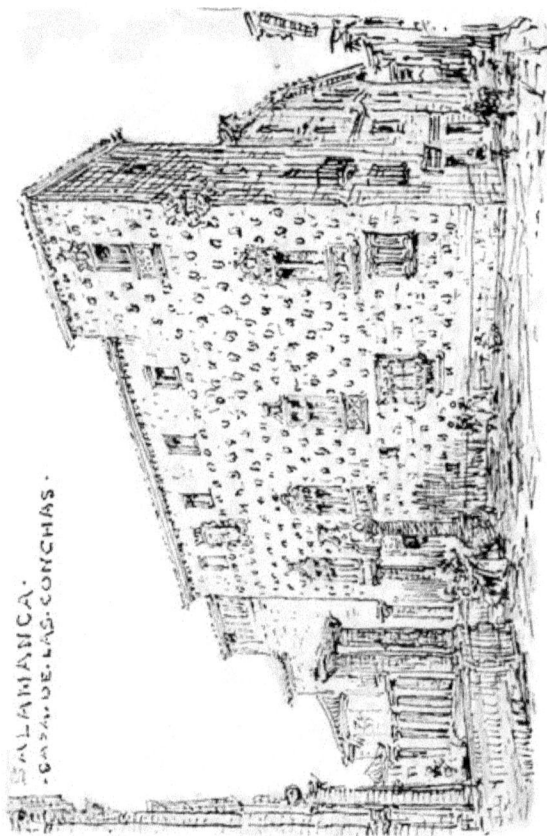

·SALAMANCA·
·CASA·DE·LAS·CONCHAS·

PLATE XIV.

—

SALAMANCA.

EXTERIOR OF THE CASA DE LAS CONCHAS.

THIS is, upon the whole, the most complete house I met with of its period, answering in Art, and nearly in point of time, to the florid Burgundian style of the Low Countries, with which there was much intercourse at the probable date of its construction—the close of the fifteenth century. It stands almost opposite the great Church of the Gesuitas, some of the columns of an unfinished porch or portico of which may be seen upon the left hand side of the sketch. No doubt this fine mansion does not possess its original roofing, as testified by the comparatively modern windows of a portion of the top storey, but with that exception it is fairly complete, both externally and internally.

The little projections on the masonry looking like nail heads are, really, as will be seen by the details given in Plates 17 and 19, representations of shells, the heraldic badge of the owner of the house, from which, rather than from his name, the cognomen by which the house is known, has been derived. It is difficult now to divine in what way the top storey was originally constructed, but judging by analogy; with what was usual in such houses elsewhere in Spain at the time, it appears probable that it may have consisted of a light open arcading, serving as a " look out"—" mirador"—and place for exercising for the ladies of the household, at times when the streets may have been neither safe nor agreeable.

SALAMANCA. CASA DE LAS CONCHAS.

PLATE XV.

—

SALAMANCA.

PATIO OF THE CASA DE LAS CONCHAS.

THE Patio of this house is yet more perfect than its façade, and, a rare circumstance in Spain, I found it both clean and well kept. It is not upon a large scale, and did not, perhaps, look the less elegant on that account. The upper arcade produces a far better effect than the lower, since in the latter the principle of the arch seems fantastically and heedlessly lost sight of. With the exception in the upper arcade of the way in which the wreaths and escutcheons are placed, as though to conceal a confusion in the lines of the archivolt, which the architect (or mason) did not seem quite to know how to bring together comfortably over the capitals, the whole effect is quiet and pretty. The open work parapet at the top is the only *motif* in the design which appears to be borrowed from the architecture of the Moors.

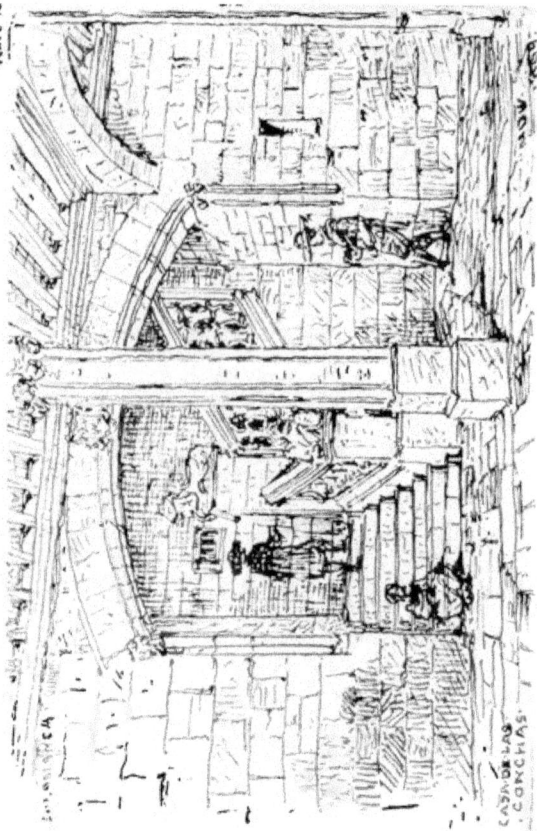

PLATE 16

SALAMANCA

CASA·DE·LAS
·CONCHAS·

PLATE XVI.

—

SALAMANCA.

STAIRCASE OF THE CASA DE LAS CONCHAS.

ON the side of the Patio, opposite to the entrance, occurs the
archway through the wall which forms the back of the
arcade on that side of the Court, and beyond which is seen the staircase
which connects the upper and lower arcades. From its masonry
bonded in with the enclosing walls, it assumes even, while simple in
design, a thoroughly architectural character, while the depth of shade,
which almost invariably covers the back wall and parts of the side
wall, serve to throw the lower part of the staircase into brilliant
relief. The graceful and gay figures which, in the characteristic
costume of Leon from time to time go up or down the staircase,
or linger upon it in groups chatting or smoking, or flirting, make
up occasional pictures, which are not rapidly effaced from the
spectator's memory.

SALAMANCA. PLATE 17

CASA DE
LAS CONCHAS

PLATE XVII.

SALAMANCA.

WINDOW FROM THE CASA DE LAS CONCHAS.

ONE of the most agreeable features in the design of the Casa de las Conchas, is the variety of detail of the different windows throughout the house. On the sketch under consideration, and in the two which follow it, evidence is afforded of the burning of this "lamp of life," as Mr. Ruskin would call it. They are all of them conceived in a transitional and composite but very picturesque style, and however different or possibly antagonistic the details of each window may appear amongst themselves, as a whole they agree and look exceedingly well.

This window occurs on the first floor of the façade, and possesses an additional interest from showing us pretty clearly what kind of windows may have been superseded in a similar situation by the Italian windows so much to be regretted in the fine Palace of the Duques del Infantado at Guadalajara. See Plate 78.

SALAMANCA
CASA DE LAS
CONCHAS

PLATE XVIII.

SALAMANCA.

WINDOW IN THE PATIO OF THE CASA DE LAS CONCHAS.

THIS window with its heavy ironwork, gives light through the back wall of the arcading of the Patio to a passage running behind a room, which derives its light from the external wall of the house. Such passages occur not unfrequently in Spanish houses, and are convenient, as they serve to bring three rooms into a suite without the necessity of having to pass through any one room to get to another. Of course of the three rooms two may be of the full width, extending from the external wall of the house to the back wall of the arcading of the Patio, and one of that width less the width of the passage, into which the three doors open, and which is lighted by a window from the Patio such as that sketched. As the Patio is a comparatively public part of the house, such windows require, and usually have, the strong close iron work, which gives security and a certain amount of privacy to the external windows of the ground-floor of the house. *—all*

and consequently approached also from the arcading by a doorway adjoining the window.

SALAMANCA

CASA·DE·LAS·
·CONCHAS·

PLATE XIX.

SALAMANCA.

EXTERNAL WINDOW OF THE CASA DE LAS CONCHAS.

THE windows of the first-floors of Spanish houses are always the largest, airiest, and openest, of the whole, excepting in the rare cases where there is a top story consisting of a large gallery, as frequently at Genoa, serving for promenade and look out—in fact a species of Belvedere. The importance of the rooms lighted is generally indicated by the relative richness of the window dressings. The profusion with which heraldic insignia are used in the window sketched, suffices, therefore, to show that with others of the same kind it lighted the principal saloons of the house. Another point of construction illustrated by the sketch, is the fact that the "conchas" or carved stone shells have been applied after the general building of the wall. This is proved by the regularity with which they are placed, irrespective of the heights of the various courses of masonry, and of the levels at which the joints occur.

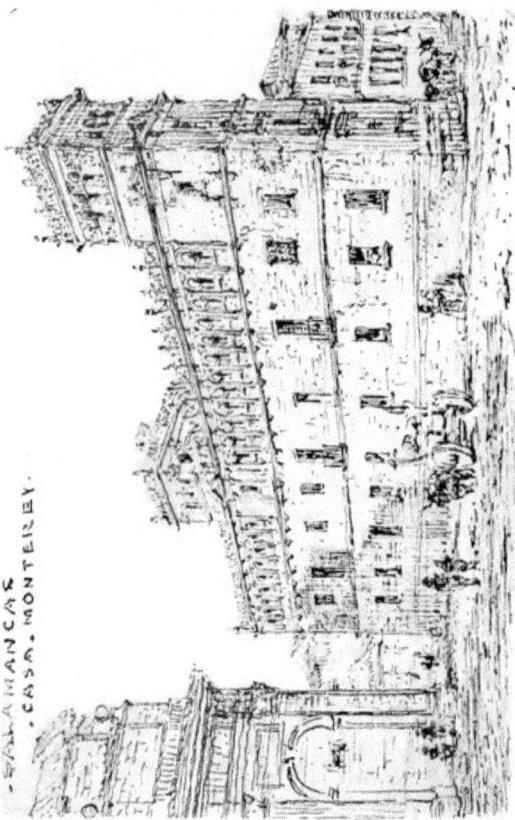

SALAMANCAS
CASA, MONTEREY.

PLATE XX.

SALAMANCA.

EXTERIOR OF THE CASA MONTEREY.

OF the very picturesque specimen of domestic architecture illustrated in Plate 20, and bearing the local name of the Casa de Monterey, but little seems to be known. Escosura confesses himself reduced to conjecture, and thus theorises on the subject. As to the exact epoch at which the Casa de Monterey was built, the following circumstances should be borne in mind. " The title of Conde de Monterey was created in favour of Don Baltasar de Zuñiga, who was Viceroy of Naples in the year 1626. This nobleman caused the Church of the Convent of Nuns which bore his name, and which stands opposite his palace, to be erected at his expense from the designs of the fashionable Italian architect, Fontana. May it be unreasonable to suppose that the Palace was designed at the same time by the same architect ?"

To this question, the ~~proper~~ answer given by some better judge of architectural style would be " very," since it is difficult to perceive any similarity between the modes of design, upon which the two buil.." are based. The architecture of the Church of the Co·· ·angle of which appears on the left hand of the sketch

florid manner of the post-Palladian Italians, while that of the Palace
is small in its ornamental parts, and instead of exhibiting Italian
features, seems throughout to show the peculiar reading of Italian
style adopted by the late Plateresque Spanish architects of the second
half of the sixteenth century. This is particularly noticeable in the
absence of a crowning balustrade, and in the substitution for it of
the elaborate pierced cresting which apparently the Spanish architects
adopted from Moorish rather than from any antique models.

The interior of this grand looking palace is said to have been all
but destroyed by the French.

SALAMANCA

OPPOSITE · SAN · BENITO.

PLATE XXI.

SALAMANCA.

RENAISSANCE HOUSE OPPOSITE SAN BENITO.

IN every ancient city the largest and most costly building ever erected in it is usually the most enduring. The causes of this are various—for instance, the construction in itself may have been the most solid, the citizens may have taken such pride in it as to bestow unusual pains upon its conservation, they may have retained it for uses for which it may have become ~~totally~~ unfit (as is the case with the majority of ancient Ecclesiastical buildings in Protestant countries), rather than face the expense of re-erecting appropriate buildings, or it may still be well suited for present purposes. Hence cathedrals, churches, palaces, (rarely castles, owing to the combative propensities of their owners), hospitals, great residences of ancient families, and in Catholic countries, convents and monasteries, of almost all periods, may remain to attest the changes of architectural style, &c.; but the ordinary residences of the middle classes, and of the numerous secondary nobility, get swept away by the tides of history, or are so altered by them as to leave scarcely any satisfactory land-marks to indicate what once gave its predominant character to the streets of many an ancient city. Such changes are effected almost equally by progress and by decay.

By the former, all minor monuments become obliterated or transformed, —they represent in fact old age, pushed aside to make way for youth—while by the latter they descend in the social scale until beggars break up what nobles once built up. How constantly the traveller meets with some splendid old cathedral still " hale and hearty," with the weight of half-a-dozen or more centuries upon its head, around which he knows were once grouped a teeming population full of strength, life, and wealth, of which not an indication may be left extending backwards for more than a hundred years from the present date? Any exceptions to such illustrations of the way in which fortune turns her wheel become the especially cherished haunts of the antiquary, who knows that from day to day they become rarer, and consequently more precious. Hence the enthusiasm with which the neglected quarters of every old town are visited in the hope of meeting with some relics of what may therein at least appear, " remains of an extinct civilization." Some such reward I met with in encountering, amidst much dirt and apparent poverty in the quarter of San Benito, in Salamanca, the pretty façades of old Renaissance houses which form the subjects of this sketch and of the one which succeeds it.

SALAMANCA.

CALLE DEL AGUILA.

PLATE XXII.

SALAMANCA.

RENAISSANCE HOUSE IN THE CALLE DEL AGUILA.

THE Renaissance house now presented to the reader, although richer in its ornaments, is not as complete as the one given in the preceding sketch, having apparently lost its original roof. Instead of the overhanging eaves casting a constantly cool shade over the open balustrading, through which light and air still pass to " a chamber that's next to the sky ;" in this case nothing is probably left over the principal apartment, the window of which richly decorated with heraldry and arabesque is shown over the strong doorway with its deep flat arch, excepting a dark and scarcely habitable attic. I think it very likely that the wreath, coat of arms, and boys, which still occupy their original position over the principal window, once supported the sill of a superior window, and that the house which now appears to have two stories only, had once at least as many as three.

Such houses as these of the ancient nobility, of which I could find only two or three, must once have been common enough in the fashionable city of Gil Blas, whose university counted its seven thousand students, and its eighty professors, with salaries of one thousand crowns each, a bountiful payment in those days for the exercise of the noblest talents, and swarms of assistants and " Pretendientes " on half-pay and unattached.*

* See Colmenar's description of the condition of the University in 1715.

AVILA
ENTRANCE TO THE
CASA
POLEN-
TINA

PLATE XXIII.

AVILA.

ENTRANCE GATEWAY OF THE CASA POLENTINA.

THE Portal which forms the subject of my twenty-third sketch serves as the entrance to the dilapidated old mansion of the Condes de Polentinos at Avila, a view of the remains of the Patio of which will be found on turning over this page. The architectural characteristics of this striking gateway are certainly very singular. On catching a glance of it from a distance, and seizing the aspect only of its ponderous masonry and deep machicolations, I fully believed I was coming upon an old bit of castellated construction of the fourteenth or fifteenth century at latest. On nearer inspection, however, I found out my mistake, and arrived at the conclusion that the Señor Conde, late in the sixteenth century, who had caused the whole structure to be built, had probably charged his architect, either to preserve the general form of some much earlier portal of the old house, which he may have caused to be pulled down, or to imitate the general aspect of some other aristocratic portal of early date, which the Count may have admired elsewhere. Different as the corbelling, &c., looks to the gateway, and the window over it, I found that ornamental detail of a similar nature to, but somewhat

coarser style than that of the door and window dressings was worked
over most of the corbelling, and part of the upper gallery carried by
the corbels, but apparently by a provincial hand.   The stone work
of the door and window had probably been left in the rough for awhile,
possibly for some fifty years, and then its carving entrusted to some
superior artist, working according to the latest lights of the fashion of
the close of the sixteenth century.   Although the style of all this
carving is plateresque, there are many indications about it of an
inclination to Greco-Roman work.   For instance, the griffins, the lions'
heads of antique type, and the arms and armour arranged as trophies,
all indicate acquaintance with the prevalent materials of Italian arabesque
design of late Cinque Cento style.   Indeed, the very form and fluting
of the corselets, brasses, vambrasses, and cuisses, would indicate that
armour of a date posterior to the middle of the sixteenth century
had been adopted as types for the making up of the trophies.

·AVILA·

·CASA·POLENTINA·

PLATE XXIV.

AVILA.

THE PATIO OF THE CASA POLENTINA.

NEXT to the general feeling of interest excited by the picturesque aspect of decayed architectural grandeur, which is presented by the remains of this dilapidated Patio, rises a feeling of curiosity as to the mode and manner of life of those whose wants such costly building subserved. Privacy and coolness appear to have been the chief desiderata, and those architectural ornaments seem to have been preferred, which recall, at almost every step, the hereditary dignities of the family tree. Madame d'Aulnois, whose Letters from Spain, written in 1679,* give the liveliest possible picture of life in those days in the Peninsula, gratifies our curiosity in the most agreeable manner, and with that quickness of perception, as to domestic habits, by means of which, none but a woman can seize at a glance, the telling details essential to give completeness and reality to a sketch. Speaking of the Spaniards of the upper and middle classes of the seventeenth century she says :—" All their houses have a great many rooms on a floor ; you go through a dozen or fifteen parlours, or chambers, one after another. Those which are the worst lodged have

* London 1771, Vol. II., page 24.

six or seven. The rooms are generally longer than they are broad'. The floors and ceilings are neither painted nor gilt ; they are made of plaister quite plain, but so white that they dazzle one's eyes; for every year they are scraped, and whited as the walls, which look like marble, they are so well polished. The Court to their summer apartments is made of certain matter, which, after it has ten pails of water thrown upon it, yet is dry in half-an-hour, and leaves a pleasant coolness ; so that in the morning they water all, and a little while after they spread mats or carpets made of fine rushes, which cover all the pavement. The whole apartments are hung with the same small mat about the depth of an ell, to hinder the coolness of the walls from hurting those which lean against them. On the top of these mats there are hung pictures and looking-glasses. The cushions, which are of gold and silver brocade, are placed upon the carpet ; and the tables and cabinets are very fine ; and at little distances there are set silver cases or boxes, filled with orange and jessamine trees. In their windows they set things made of straw, to keep the sun out ; and in the evenings they work in their gardens. There are several houses which have very fine ones, where you see grotto's and fountains in abundance."

·AVILA·

·THE·CATHEDRAL·   ·IRON·PULPIT·

PLATE XXV.

AVILA.

IRON PULPIT IN THE CATHEDRAL.

MR. STREET'S illustrations and description of all that is left of the old glories of Avila, previous to the epoch of the Renaissance, are so complete, that I can feel no compunction in having gleaned only from this delightful old city two specimens of the ability of the Spanish smiths of the period he repudiates, and two others showing remains of the domestic architecture of the same style.

Let it not be supposed, however, that it was only the school of the Renaissance which produced masterly iron-work, and even masterly iron pulpits, in Spain. Mr. Street has himself given us a beautiful woodcut of the pulpit in the church of St. Gil, at Burgos. This exhibits no other than Gothic details, while in the pulpit which forms the subject of my twenty-fifth sketch, as will no doubt be observed, Renaissance details are freely intermixed with Gothic ones. The whole, however different in style in different parts, appeared to me to be contemporaneous ; and I, therefore, regard this pulpit as an interesting example of a transitional style, later of course, than that followed in the pulpit of Saint Gil, which Mr. Street describes as the earliest he saw. In both, the primitive mode of working through superposed thin plates to form tracery has been adhered to, and the whole of the ironwork has been applied to a wooden framework. I regard the pulpit at Burgos as likely to have been executed early in the fifteenth century, and the one now under consideration as of the close of the same century; and both may, I think, have been produced under the influence of the masters from Cologne, who did such wonders, and set so many fashions, in Burgos and its vicinity, of course, especially at Miraflores.

·AVILA·
THE CATHEDRAL

PLATE XXVI.

AVILA.

IRON PULPIT IN THE CATHEDRAL.

IN method of manufacture no less than in style of design this pulpit, which forms a pendant to the one last given just outside the choir of Avila Cathedral, offers a contrast to its predecessor. We no longer meet with a superposition of perforated plates, but the operations of beating and chasing, and, indeed, cutting the metal with chisels, files and hammers; working in fact as the Italians term it "a massiccio." The basis of the design is no longer Gothic, but strictly of the regular Spanish Plateresque Renaissance with balustrade columns, figures in niches, and Arabesques imitated from the Italians. From all these details, we may fairly be justified in ascribing this work to about the middle of the sixteenth century.

The method of working this pulpit is no longer that of the simple smith, but really corresponds much more closely with that of the armourer which reached its zenith about this period. There can be no doubt that the Spaniards gained much of their well-known skill in the manipulation of iron and steel from the Moors, who had themselves obtained knowledge from Damascus, and perhaps even improved upon the knowledge they had derived from that source. From the times of the

Carthaginians and Romans, the Celt-Iberian mines had been known as amongst the richest existing sources, from which iron could be procured. Many fragments of finely wrought iron work, of the middle ages, still exist in Spain ; but for the most part in very fragmentary condition.* From the end of the fifteenth century, however, in the Rejas, great seats and the screens, (such as that seen at the back of the pulpit in my sketch) of the churches and cathedrals, and especially in the arms and armour of Moorish and Christian Caballeros as attested by many splendid specimens in the Real Armeria of Madrid, perfect examples are to be met with of the skill of Spanish artificers in dealing with all the metallurgical processes by which iron and steel can be made to assume forms of grace and beauty. Charles V., Philip II., and Don Juan of Austria, were boundless in their extravagance in the encouragement of the best armourers, not of Toledo and Valladolid only, but of Milan and Augsburg as well. There can be no doubt that the models of beauty bought by these Sovereigns from artists in iron and steel, such as the Negroli and Piccinini, tended to develope that perfection of workmanship, which was attained in Spain in the reign of Philip III. The pains-taking editors of the Catalogue of the Madrid Armoury cite Pamplona as at the head of the trade at the close of the sixteenth and beginning of the seventeenth centuries, and name as the chief rivals to Pamplona of the cities of Spain, in the manufacture of splendid arms and armour, Tolosa, Barcelona, and Calatayud.*

* There is much in this very town of Avila in the beautiful old church of San Vicente.

† Catalogo de la Real Armeria—siendo Director General, &c.—el S. D. José Maria Marchesi —Madrid, 1849, pages 188-89.

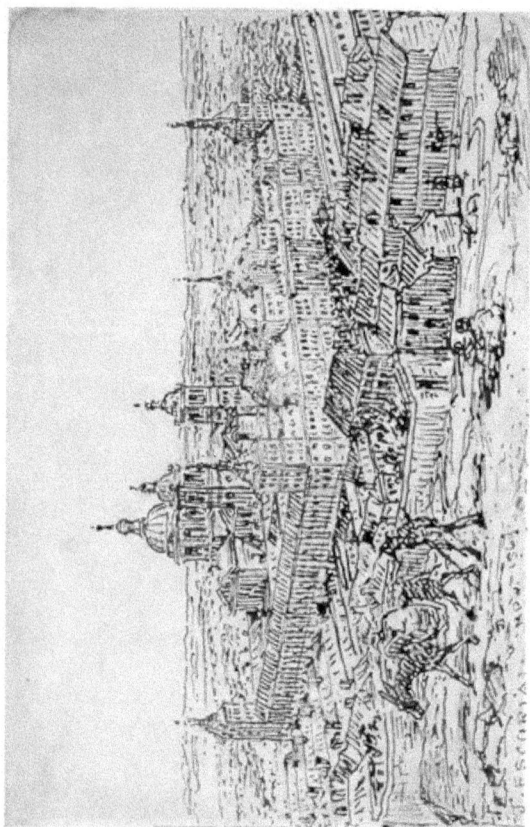

EL ESCORIAL DESDE EL MONTE

PLATE XXVII.

ESCORIAL.

GENERAL VIEW OF THE ESCORIAL.

IN all Spain I saw nothing which so ill-agreed with my preconceptions as the Escorial. As for beauty, I could find none whatever in it. The building appeared to me thoroughly unsatisfactory alike as church, palace, or monastery. Still, to omit it altogether from any series of Spanish sketches with pen or pencil, would be to leave out the Monument which reflects, probably, more perfectly than any other in the Peninsula, the mixture of arrogant extravagance, and arid asceticism, which characterized its most potent rulers in the plenitude of their historical importance. In it, in my opinion, Herrera proved himself an architect thoroughly worthy of the masters who employed him, formal, pedantic, cold, extravagant to a degree, and yet mean. That the building contains many most interesting works of art, is as true, as that a visit to it should on no account be omitted by any one who would at all attempt to realize what the Spanish Court may have been in the days of Philip II.; but, after all, I am bound to confess that what most pleased me in the vast edifice, with the exception of some few pictures and illuminated books, was the work of Italians and not of Spaniards, viz., the marble crucifix of Benvenuto Cellini, the magnificent

gilt bronze statues of the Kings and Queens of Spain in the Church,
by Pompeio Leoni, and the decorations of the Library, principally by
Pelegrino Tibaldi. To such a judgment may be objected that the
structure now is not what it was, let us see what an acute observer says
of it, writing late in the seventeenth century :—

"A while after we went to the Escurial, which to give it no less
than its due, may in Spain pass for an admirable structure, but where
building is understood, would not be looked on as very extraordinary.
In a general consideration, it seems a mass of stone of great perfection ;
but going to particulars, scarce any of them but falls very short of
the magnificence imagined, and that so much, that if Philip the Second,
who built it, and was called the Solomon of his age, did no more
resemble that wise king then this edifice does his Temple, to which it
is often compared, the copy comes very short of the original ; in the
meantime to stretch the comparison they please themselves in saying,
that Charles the Fifth, like another David, only designed his holy work,
which (being a man of war and blood) God reserved for his son.
Ignorant strangers are entertained with this tale, but such as are versed
in history tell us, that after the battle of St. Quentin, Philip the Second
made two vows, one never to go in person to the wars, the other to build
this cloyster for the Order of St. Jerome instead of that which had
been burnt, it cost him near six millions of gold, though out of
consideration of parsimony and convenience of bringing stone, he made
choice of the worst situation in nature, for it is at the foot of a barren
mountain, and hard by a wretched village called Escurial, that can hardly
lodge a man of any fashion; this may seem very strange to those that
know the Court is there twice in a year : the place it stands on is, by
transcendence, called the Seat, because it was levelled in order to build on.

"The fabrick is very fair, with four towers at the four corners, but coming to it, one knows not which way to enter, for as soon as out of the great walk, in a kind of Piazza, you see only little doors, which, when you are over it, lead into two pavilions, that contain offices and lodgings for some of the Court; when you have well viewed this side of the square, you come to that which is towards the mountain, where there is a very large magnificent portal, on each side beautify'd with pillars; by this stately gate you enter a quadrangle, where right over against it stands the Church, ascended to it by a stair of five or six steps, as long as the Court is large, extending from one side of it to the other, very fair columnes support the porch, and on the top of the wall stand six statues, the middlemost of which are David and Solomon, by whom they would represent Charles the Fifth, and Philip the Second. About the church are many pavillions, all comprehended in the exact square which environs that building. Report mentions many Bascourts, but we could not reckon above seven or eight. That this is a very fair cloyster for Friers cannot be denied, neither can it be allowed to be a pallace magnificent enough for such a monarch as Philip the Second, who having built it in one and-twenty years, and enjoyed it twelve or thirteen, boasted, that from the foot of a mountain and his closet, with two inches of paper, he made himself obeyed in the Old and New World.

"The King and Queen's apartments have nothing in them that appears roial, they are altogether unfurnished, and they say, when the King goes to any of his houses of pleasure, they remove all to the very bedsteads; the rooms are little and low; the roofs not beautiful enough to invite the eyes to look up to them; its many pictures of excellent masters, and especially of Titian, that wrought a great while there,

are very much vaunted, yet there are not so many as report gives out.
The Spaniards have so little understanding of pictures, they are alike
taken with all, and the Marquis Serragenovese, that accompanied us,
sufficiently laughed at the foolishness of a Castillian, who, willing to
have us admire the slightest and wretchedest landskipes of a gallery
where we were, told us nothing could equalize them, because in a
place where their King sometimes walked. There are yet in the vestry
some good pieces, especially a Christ, and Mary Magdalen; and in
the Church others very estimable. For paintings in fresco, the quire,
done by Titian, is doubtlessly an excellent work, and so is the library,
I think by the same hand, where amongst the rest is represented the
ancient Roman manner of defending criminals, who stand by bound
hand and foot; Cicero is also there pleading for Milo, or some other,
I not being sufficiently acquainted with his meen, to be positive, and
without apprehension of mistaking; this library is truly very
considerable, as well for its length, breadth, height, and light; the
pictures and marble tables that stand in the midst of it, as for its
quantity of choice and rare books, if we may believe the monks; they
are certainly very well bound and guilded, and if I mistake not, but
seldom read. In the vestry, they show priests' copes, where embroidery
and pearl with emulation contend whether art or matter renders them
more rich and sumptuous; they showed us a cross of very fair pearl,
diamonds, and emeralds; it is a very pretty knack, and would not
become less such if it changed countreys, I would willingly have
undertaken for it if they would have suffered it to pass the Pyreneans,
had it been only to show my friends a hundred thousand crowns in
a nut-shell. The library I have spoken of, the high altar and
monument of their kings, which they call Pantheon (though I know

not why, unless because a single round arch like the Pantheon at Rome), are certainly the best pieces of this magnificent fabrick. The high altar is approached by steps of red marble, and invironed by sixteen pillars of jasper, which reach the top of the quire, and cost only a matter of fifty or sixty thousand crowns cutting, between these are niches with statues of guilded brass, and so there are on the side of the tables and praying places. The Pantheon is under the altar, and descended by stairs, though narrow, very light; at the entrance of this rich chappel, a marble shines, whose lustre is heightened by reflexion of the gold, with which all the iron-work and part of that fair stone are overlaid. In the middle of it, and right against the altar, is a fair candlestick of brass, gilded, and in six several niches, twenty-four sepulchres of black marble to receive as many bodies; above the gate are two more. This stately monument is small, but sumptuous, it was finished by the present King, who, about six months since placed there the bodies of Charles the Fifth, Philip the Second, and Philip the Third. The first was most intire; in the niches, on the left, lie the Queens, and the last of them Queen Elizabeth of Burbon. He that preached the day that these seven tombs or sepulchres had bodies laid in them, began by his apprehension to speak in presence of so many kings who had conquered the world, and expressed himself so well, and so highly pleased the King that he got a yearly pension of a thousand crowns. Nothing attaining such perfection as to secure it from the teeth of criticks, the three pieces I have now mentioned, have been attacqued by them. It is objected against the Library, that its entrance suits not with its magnificence and grandeur, and that it stands as if stoln in, and not of the same piece with the rest.

"Over against the great altar, where all is so well proportioned, they wish away a silver lamp, whose size corresponds not with that of the place it burns in, which is vast and large. In the Pantheon they find great fault, that all the steps by which it is descended are not marble, and that the sides of the walls are not incrusted with it, the chappel being all so, and a like magnificence requisite everywhere. In the brazen candlestick, the inner part which is not guilded is discerned amongst the black and foul branches that extend from it. It cost ten thousand crowns, which is ten times more than it is worth; but it is common in this country to boast things of excessive price, which they would have admired on that account, as if because they are foolish merchants, the ware they buy too dear, were therefore the more valuable. These are my observations of the so famous Escurial, adorned only by some small parterras and fountains; one side of it affords a handsome prospect, but the ground near it is the greatest part rock or heath, some walks and groves are planted about it, but being cold and windy, trees thrive not. There are some deer in a kind of park, ill-designed, and with very low walls, the way to it is nothing pleasant, and the King who goes thither thrice every year, one of which times is in the winter, cannot certainly find any great diversion in those journeys, for during three months all is covered with snow."

Nothing need be added, I think, to so graphic a "boutade" as this, which, though somewhat satirical, would not appear to have been much too highly coloured for the occasion.

SEGOVIA

PLATE XXVIII.

SEGOVIA.

GATEWAY IN THE CITY WALLS.

THERE is probably no city in all Spain, and few perhaps in any part of the world, in which within a similar compass, so many good, although fragmentary, materials could be found for illustrating styles and inflections of style in building, from the days of the Romans through those of the Moors and Christians, up to the period of the Renaissance, than Segovia. Of this last named period, two of the greatest masters, Gil de Ontañon and his son Rodrigo, have nobly left their mark in the splendid Cathedral, a worthy rival to that of Salamanca, also executed from the designs, and under the personal superintendence of the elder of the two Ontañones. The city, probably, owes these varied monuments to its merits, as a strong, as well as a beautiful position. Under these circumstances, it is not to be wondered at that its old walls should offer many features of interest as well as picturesqueness. In fact, to the educated eye, the former is almost a necessary ingredient to making up the latter. As I wended my way upwards, therefore, from the railway station to the town, through this gateway, about which I caught indications here of one style, and there of another, Roman, Moor, and Christian doing here a jot and there a little, that I should linger on my way for awhile; partly, perhaps, to cool myself, and partly to make the little sketch I present herewith to my readers.

I need, perhaps, only add that the rough but effective cornice of the gateway is made up from its top to its bottom by different combinations of common tiles, and that its little enriched frieze is a specimen of the clever stucco-work, probably executed by workmen of Moorish descent in Renaissance times. The whole, even to the painting of the Virgin, is roughly executed, but is not the less graceful, perhaps, from the apparent absence of all effort. An aspect of spontaneity in works of art has its own particular charm, as has the semblance of the most careful solicitude under appropriate circumstances. The true artist, heedful of his "when" and "how," is master of both moods.

SEGOVIA

THE ALCAZAR.   HALL OF THE KINGS.

SEGOVIA.

ARCHWAY IN THE HALL OF THE KINGS.

DON Juan Alvarez de Colmenar[*] writing at the commencement of the eighteenth century gives the following description of the Royal Palace at Segovia—

"The Alcazar," he says, "is situated on a mountain in the highest part of the city. It is entirely covered with lead; the access to it being by means of a staircase cut in the rock. There is always a sentinel in the towers, and on a platform may be seen many cannons of which the greater number are pointed against the city, and the residue towards the faubourg and country. It contains sixteen richly tapestried chambers one of which has a fireplace of porphyry. Thence a descent may be made to another platform smaller than the first mentioned also furnished with cannon. From this, access is obtained to a small chamber with gilt dado, marble fireplace, and walls covered with mirrors up to the ceiling. Near this room is the Royal Chapel splendidly gilt and decorated with very fine pictures, amongst which that of the Magi is of the highest beauty. Issuing from the chapel is a magnificent hall gilt from

* Les Délices de l'Espagne et du Portugal—Leide chez Pierre van der Aa, 1706.

top to bottom. It is called the Sala de los Reyes, "(literary the Hall of the Kings,)" because therein are all the Kings of Spain from Pelayo to Jane, mother of the Emperors Charles V. and Ferdinand. They are represented seated on thrones under canopies so artistically worked that they look like agates. There is another hall lined with glasses of the height of three feet with marble seats and ceilings gilt with pure gold. All these halls are differently ornamented, and with the exception of the gilding there is not one like the others. The river which surrounds the château forms its moat."*

I have preferred quoting this old description to giving one of the present aspect of this once splendid palace, since of all its magnificence nothing is now left but its massive walls covered here and there with the elegant stucco-work some of which is given in my sketches, and its commanding and noble position which is one of very great natural strength. Here it was that the Moors, who never failed to fortify such spots, reared the great central tower around which, after its capture by the Christians, the Spanish sovereigns built the palace which contained the majority of the apartments described by Colmenares, employing the sub-jugated Moorish artificers for many of the original decorations. In 1412, a splendid hall called, from its celebrated ceiling, the Sala del Arteson, was completed, as testified by an inscription to that effect given at length by Cean Bermudez.† Other inscriptions mark the work executed by the king, Henry IV. in 1452, 1456, and 1458,

---

* See the true and topographical views given in the above work, and the artistic and considerably embellished one by David Roberts in Jennings' Landscape Annual for 1837.

† "Documentos," Vol. I. of the "Noticias" Appendix No. xxxviii.

who resided in it amidst his treasures, and the glorious spoils taken
in what one inscription designates "la guerra de los Moros."
Here dwelt Isabella la Catolica, and at a later date Charles V.
The decorations described by Colmenares were probably for the
most part those executed by command of Philip II., the elegant stucco
work given in the sketch (No. 29) being clearly of the time of
Henry IV. Here lodged our Charles I. in 1623. The wretched
Philip V. with congenial propriety converted it into a prison,
justifying Le Sage's amusing sketch of the committal to it of Gil Blas.
Many of the Algerine and Barbary pirates taken by the Spanish
men-of-war were here confined. At length it was converted into
an academy for artillery cadets, and made a miserable sort of
Woolwich. Decorations were torn down, old windows blocked up,
and new ones made in the most barbarous style. Stoves were placed
in most dangerous situations, until as a natural consequence a fire
broke out, and the "coup de grâce" was given to the glories of
this palatial fortress, which is now alike useless for royal, military,
or civic purposes.

PLATE XXX.

SEGOVIA.

DETAIL FROM THE ALCAZAR.

IN describing the last sketch (No. 29), some particulars were given of the building from which both that and this (No. 30) were taken. It may be well to note now the peculiar style of design illustrated by both. This style is what is technically known in Spain as "Mudejar," *i.e.*, neither Gothic nor Moorish strictly, but a compound of both. The date of these particular specimens happens to be well fixed by the inscriptions to which allusion has been recently made, and of one of which a portion is shown in the sketch (No. 30), as running horizontally between two string courses on each side of the small quasi-rose windows. This "Mudejar" work was certainly executed between the years 1452 and 1458, in the reign of Enrique IV., King of Castille. It was the wise policy of the most sagacious of the Spanish monarchs in their contests with the Moors, to half-shut their eyes to what they could not eradicate, viz., the secret Islamism of the race. They long continued this laudable inclination to tolerate and use the skilful Arabian artificers, under Christian guidance and superintendence, in the various localities in which they successively planted the Standard of the Cross, tearing down that of the Crescent. At last the

inflation which followed their ultimate conquests under Ferdinand and
Isabella, led to the establishment of the pernicious Inquisition, the
"teterrima causa" of infinite misery, and the subverter of tolerance
and progress throughout the country. From that period gradually
disappeared, lingering, as we shall have occasion to observe, much
longer in the South than in the North, the skilled artificer, learned in
all the technicalities, and the elaborate geometrical principles of the
combination of ornamental form, which Arabian genius had engrafted
upon the traditions of Ancient Rome, handed down to them through
the medium of Byzantium. The very antagonism of creed induced the
Moor to avoid polluting his art with types of form or processes
borrowed from the Christian, as he would have avoided polluting his
faith with Catholic legend or tenets. Hence when he and his became the
spoil of the Christian, which, to a great extent, they did, the Christian
necessarily inherited no unimportant addition to his repertory of
beautiful, fresh, and valuable arts and industries. This precious
inheritance was not altogether appreciated by the Spaniards, as it might
have been by a people of greater producing energies; but in spite of
their comparative ineptitude, they gained greatly by the leaven of
Moorish skill and talent; and as one of the first and best fruits of the
gradual conquest and absorption of the race, we may certainly reckon
the leading features of the " Mudejar " style.

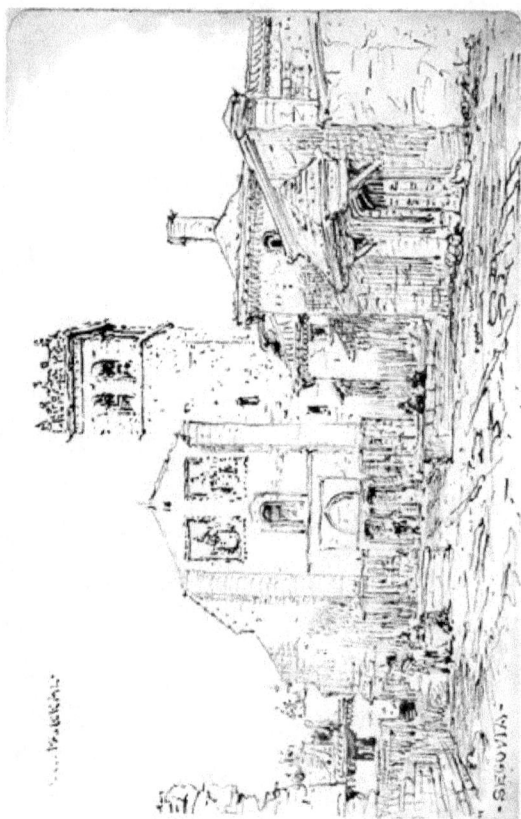

SEGOVIA

PLATE XXXI.

SEGOVIA.

EXTERIOR VIEW OF THE MONASTERY OF EL PARRAL.

N Mr. Street's work on "Gothic Architecture on Spain," so justly
praised by all who know anything of ancient Spanish Art will be
found on Plate VIII a sketch plan, and on pages 185 and 186 a full
description of this extensive old Convent, and especially of the Church
of the Vera Cruz to which it is attached. I felt, therefore, that my
duty to the student would be best fulfilled by simply laying before
him a sketch of the exterior to supplement Mr. Street's ground plan,
referring the student for all further information to his work. It would
have been easy to extract from Cean Bermudez the same historical
details; but it could only have resulted in a thrice told tale. It may
suffice to note that the entrance to the Convent may be sought (with
much but rarely effectual knocking and ringing) through the curious
old porch represented in my sketch on the right hand of the Church,
which should be visited in the morning, on account of its beautiful
arrangement of lighting, mainly from the East.

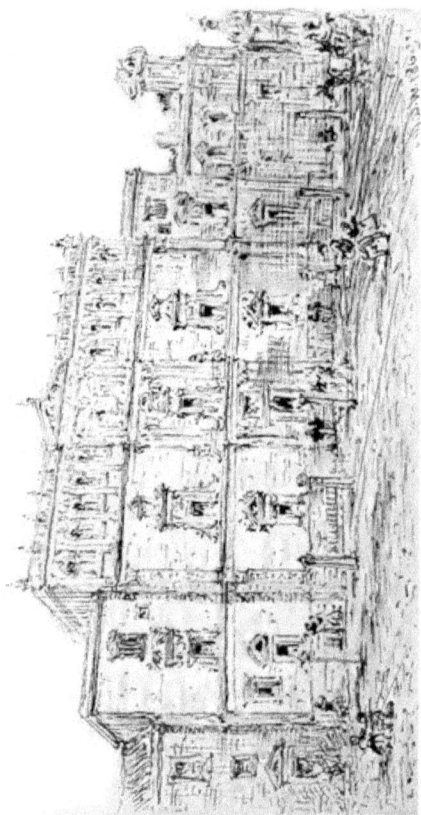

· ALCALA · DE · HENARES ·   · COLEGIO · DE · SAN · ILDEFONSO ·

PLATE XXXII.

ALCALA-DE-HENARES.

EXTERIOR OF THE COLEGIO DE SAN ILDEFONSO.

SUCH a man as Francis Ximenez de Cisneros—the founder of the University at Alcala de Heñares—would have been a man amongst men anywhere; but in Spain, his union of prudence with strength, courage with calmness, learning in the closet with action in the field, humility with aptitude for supreme command, benevolence with the sternest energy, raised him rapidly from poverty and insignificance to the Regency of that country. So aggrandized he ruled the kingdom for many years, until his death, in 1517, with far greater wisdom, and more to the benefit of the State, than any Sovereign who has ever sat upon its throne. This is not the place in which to dwell upon his life, intensely interesting as it was, but only to briefly allude to the relics of his greatness as displayed in Alcala de Heñares, in which locality he himself commenced his studies. Protected by Mendoza he became confessor to Isabella in 1492, who made him Archbishop of Toledo in 1495. Three years afterwards he founded his great University dedicated to Saint Ildefonso; but which, in honour of his ever famous labour, the compilation of the Complutensian Polyglot,*

* Printed at Alcala in 1514-15 in 6 vols. folio.

bears the distinguished name in Spain of the " Universidad Complutense."

The building, of which the main block of the façade shown in my sketch, is about one hundred feet long, by about sixty-five feet high, contains no less than three Patios of different styles. It was designed by Pedro Gumiel, and, as originally planned, finished in 1533, by Rodrigo Gil. The whole façade which is of marble, with the exception of the basement of grey granite, was no doubt entirely the work of the last named architect. The structure has been well illustrated, architecturally, in the great government publication—the " Monumentos Arquitectonicos de España"—to which the student may be referred for the details of this immense establishment. About it, in the days of its full prosperity, there were grouped no less than eleven thousand students, and nineteen colleges. Nothing shows, perhaps, more clearly the " high estate " from which the poor Spain of the present day has fallen, than a contrast between the muster rolls of the University of Madrid, of late years, and those of Salamanca, and Alcala, in the Sixteenth Century.

The visitor to the " Colegio " of Alcala should on no account omit to see the chapel built by Gil de Ontañon, since within it rests the Wolsey of Spain. Upon a monument of white marble, by the skilful hand of Domenico of Florence, reposes an effigy of Cardinal Cisneros. A lithograph of this and of the quasi-Mudejar style of the chapel is given in the work of Villa Amil,* and we may well take to heart the concluding sentence of the description of it by Patricio Escosura :—
"Una pregunta, y concluimos ; ¿ Guantos monumentos como el que acabamos de ejaminar dejarémos nosotros en herencia à nuestros nietos ?"

* España Artistica y monumental de Villa Amil y Escosura, Vol. I. page 82.

PLATE XXXIII.

ACALA DE HEÑARES.

WINDOW OF THE ARZOBISPADO.

HE Archi-episcopal Palace of Alcala de Heñares is a building of many periods and many styles. Founded upon the Old Alcazar, of which vestiges remain, it contains several pretty mediæval windows, one of which Mr. Street thought not unworthy of his pencil. The late plateresque details of its double Patios arrested my attention, and I was pleased to observe in them a more than usual elegance of moulding, and originality, with propriety of style. On account of their possession of these qualities, their invention and the execution of the medallion-heads and ornaments have been ascribed to Alonzo Berraguete, whose studies in Florence have been looked upon as the main agents in purifying the then prevalent tendency to exuberance in Plateresque design to which he might have surrendered himself, but for his opportunities of becoming acquainted with the works of Michael Angelo and other great contemporary masters of Italian Art. If Berruguete had no hand in this work, (and I have been able to find no proof whatever that he had), it lends greater probability to the theory I have ventured to broach in the description of the next sketch, which is taken from another but contemporary part of the same building.

Another attribution of the design of these details has been to Alonso de Covarrubias, but I can find no other authority for it than the fact that Ponz considered them to resemble certain windows of the Alcazar at Toledo which were known to have been designed by that master.

ALCALA DE HENARES

PLATE XXIV. ~~X~~

32.

ALCALA DE HEÑARES.

DETAIL FROM THE ARYOBISPADO.

ALTHOUGH commonly described as Plateresque, the architecture of the Patio of the Archbishop's Palace at Alcala de Heñares, of which my sketch represents the detail of the upper storey, excites a far more forcible reminiscence of good Cinque-Cento work. It seems to have been executed no doubt principally, by Spaniards of the sixteenth century, but still to have been founded on pure Italian models. This is particularly shown, as it appeared to me, in the regular form of the bell and volutes of the capitals of the columns with the well drawn and cut acanthus leaves, and the regular eggs and tongues of the cornice. Recognising this, and noticing the correspondence in style between the execution of this work, and that of the architectural parts of the monument to the Great Cardinal alluded to in the description of the last sketch but one, I could not but fancy it possible that the same artist, Domenico of Florence, who is allowed to have produced that monument, may, after its completion, have been retained to work upon the Patios of the Archi-episcopal Palace; and possibly also upon some portions of the façade of the University which was not as we know set in hand until some time after the Cardinal's death.

. TOLEDO .

PLATE 35.

TOLEDO.

VIEW OF THE REMAINS OF A MOORISH FORTRESS ON THE RIVER.

HE situation of Toledo is most romantic, and presents as many charms as the site for a commanding city, from its beauty to the architect, as no doubt it offered from, its great natural strength, to the "man of war" who naturally regarded it as an almost heaven-born fortress. It owes much, both of its beauty and its strength, to the clear and abundant current of the Tagus, which more than half surrounds it. This river has, as we shall have occasion to observe, been nobly spanned by Roman, Moor, and Christian ; and on its banks are yet traceable, in architectural fragments, the handiwork of each of those races.

Our sketch represents a passage of this river which has once been commanded by the Moorish fortress, above the "tapia" or concrete remains of which, some shade-loving Spaniard of to-day has planted his vines and gourds, and reared his modest, but neither unpicturesque nor altogether uncomfortable, tenement. A fortification of this kind was much affected by the Moors for salient points, on account of the command it gave them of the various directions from which attack might be apprehended, and was called by them "Almodovar."

Charles Didier has admirably described the charms of such a position, as that occupied by the world-renowned capital of New Castille, in the following passage of his "Année en Espagne," "Tolède doit à sa situation," says he,[*] "une inépuisable richesse de sites et de vues. La montagne escarpée dont elle couvre les flancs est séparée par le Tage d'une autre montagne non moins escarpée, mais nue, déserte, abandonée à la stérilité et tombant à pic dans le fleuve. A mi-côte est le château ruiné de Saint Cervantes. Un petit ermitage, _la Virgen del Valle_, est égaré au sommet ; mais, bâti au milieu des rochers, il s'en détache à peine et se confond avec eux : des troupeaux de chèvres sauvages errent à l'entour, et, presque aussi sauvage qu'elles, le pâtre, vêtu de peaux, apporte au seuil de la ville les mœurs de la sierra. Ces contrastes sont frappants, mais ce sont les vues surtout qui captivent ; quoique borné, le spectacle est varié ; les masses granitiques dont la montagne est formée s'adoucissent au-dessus du pont Saint Martin, et des villas, appelées dans le pays _cigarrales_, étendent sur la pierre nue et grisâtre de frais tapis de verdure ; c'est le seul point champêtre du paysage, tout le reste est sec et dépouillé. La montagne n'a pas un arbre. La variété naît des mouvements du sol et des anfractuosités du rocher ; les perspectives sont courtes, mais frappantes ; tantôt l'œil plonge sur le Tage, qui serpente en méandres verdâtres entre les deux collines ; tantôt la ville apparaît hérissée de ses innombrables clochers, puis le rideau retombe, et enferronné dans une gorge déserte et muette, on pourrait se croire tout d'un coup transporté dans quelque solitude primitive. Ces brusques alternatives ont un grand charme ; elles impriment à ce paysage austère et mélancolique un profond cachet d'originalité."

[*] Tome I., page 222. Bruxelles, 1837.

TOLEDO: BRIDGE OF ALCANTARA

PLATE XXXVI.

TOLEDO.

BRIDGE OF ALCANTARA.

/ HE brief words in which Ford gives the chronology of this
"Bridge of Bridges" carries one to the long series of Lords
and Masters who have made of Toledo a perfect mine of Archæological
interest. "The Roman one," he says, "was repaired in 687 by
the Goth Sala; destroyed by an inundation, it was rebuilt in 871,
by the Alcaide Halaf, repaired in 1258 by Alonzo el Sabio,* restored
by Archbishop Tenorio about 1380, and fortified in 1484 by Andres
Manrique." To crown the whole and make it safe for ever, Philip
II. placed it, by solemn dedication, under the especial protection of
San Ildefonso, who certainly appears to have done his duty hitherto,
as I saw few signs of repair or want of it from the middle of the
sixteenth century till now. I need scarcely say, that it crosses the
River Tagus in one noble and most lofty span, and connects the
walled city with its dependencies "across the water." Nothing can
be more picturesque than this bridge, or indeed the whole aspect of

---

* The greater part of the above facts are verified by the inscription which was placed upon
the bridge by Alonzo the Wise, in 1252, and the original of which is given by Cean Bermudez
in his "Documentos" Vol. I. Number XXIV.

the position of the city placed upon seven hills, forming one lofty and
rocky eminence, around which on more than two sides, tears the
Tagus. Conspicuous in my sketch is the lofty Tower controlling
access from the Bridge to the City on the side of the commanding
" Alcazar " as literally the royal residence," as Alcantara is in Arabic
" the Bridge." Cean Bermudez* tells us, that one Mateo Paradiso
was the architect, who in 1217 constructed a tower (probably, in at
least the greatest part, the same which now remains) upon this famous
bridge. In support of his opinion, he cites Estévan de Garibay, who
in the ninth volume of his " unedited Works " fol. 512 tit. 6°, speaking
of the Memorabilia of Toledo, says with reference to this Bridge,
" that the river suddenly rising destroyed one of its pillars in the
month of February, 1211, placing the bridge in peril of falling. As
soon as it had been repaired, Henrique I. caused a tower to be built
upon it for the greater security of it and of the city as appears by an
original inscription which once existed upon the tower in these
words."

"Henry, son of the King Alfonso, caused this tower to be built in honour of God, by the
hand of Matheo Paradiso in the year 1255."

Another tower of the time of Charles V. guards the access to
the Bridge from the side farthest from the city, that from which my
sketch has been taken.

* Noticias de los Arquitectos, &c. Par Amirola y Bermudez, Madrid, 1829. Vol. I page 41.

PLATE 27

PLATE XXXVII.

TOLEDO.

BRIDGE OF SAN MARTIN.

AMIROLA* has given us an excellent acount of the origin of this
noble mediæval bridge, upon which the following short
statement is mainly based. Near to the site on which the bridge of
St. Martin now stands at Toledo, there was formerly a fine Roman
bridge. This having been entirely destroyed for useful purposes, by
a tremendous flood which rose, according to the most ancient annals of
Toledo, in the year 1212, the city determined upon building another
bridge upon a better site. Having erected abutments of vast strength,
which were ultimately crowned and weighted with two towers for
defence, and having bedded two solid piers in the line of the stream,
their master of the works, Rodrigo Alfonso, proceeded to span it with
one of three lofty arches, two of which are shown in my sketch.
This magnificent arch of one hundred and forty Spanish feet in width,
and ninety-five in height was destroyed in the terrible struggle between
the King Don Pedro, and his brother Don Henrique, in the year 1368.
It was shortly after rebuilt, and the bridge generally repaired by the
great Don Tenorio, Archbishop of Toledo. Villa Franca, Alcala de

* Noticias &c. Vol. I. page 79.

Heñares, and the neighbourhood of Alamin, all boasted of bridges put up by the same Rodrigo Alfonso, who designed the bridge of San Martin at Toledo.

Beyond the bridge, in my sketch, appears on the crest of the hill the mass of the beautiful, though somewhat over florid church, San Juan de los Reyes. Having been erected by Ferdinand and Isabella, in a period as late as 1476, it fails to enlist the sympathies and approbation of some; other writers have praised it enthusiastically, and certain it is, that if it may have possessed faults when complete, scarcely any thing can be more picturesque as a ruin.

TOLEDO   MDCCLXXV

MW 1809
MOORISH GATEWAY BY BRIDGE OF ALCANTARA

PLATE XXXVIII.

TOLEDO.

MOORISH GATEWAY BY THE BRIDGE OF ALCANTARA.

NEAR to the bridge of Alcantara (sketch No. 36) on the road leading up from it to the city, stands the celebrated Moorish gateway of the " Puerta del Sol." This strong, large, and well fortified approach to the city, I found to labour under two marked disadvantages for my sketch-book, viz., it had been too often illustrated, and its curious details had been so vigorously " restored " (when Spaniards do "restore" there is no mistake about it), as to have lost in a great degree the characteristics of originality and dependability. I looked about, therefore, in the immediate vicinity of the bridge, for other vestiges of the antiquity of the city. These I soon came upon in the old gateway of which I give a sketch, and to the construction of which, both Roman and Moor have contributed. As the poor heavily laden mules laboured up the dusty stony road, with the patience of, in Spain, a much-abused race, it was impossible not to speculate upon the generations upon generations which had followed in the same track up the same road, on the same duty, through every vicissitude of occupation of the Gateway, through which they swayed monotonously from side to side.

TOLEDO.

PLATE XXXIX.

TO / EDO.

ENTRANCE ARCHWAY OF THE ZOCODOVER.

ALTHOUGH as appears from the steps shown in my sketch rising up through this archway, which is known as that of the Zocodover, or more properly Zocodober, which means in Arabic, according to Cean Bermudez, "a place upon a lower level," the archway is situated upon an *ascent*, it by no means follows that there may not be a higher plane to which it may be still a descent. Such is the case in the Zocodover of Toledo, which is really the " Place " of the city in the usual French, or the " Piazza " in the Italian / sense. It is reached from without the walls by the steps shown, and is yet literally the " lower Place " when compared with the platform of the Alcazar or " Royal Residence." Of great strength, it must in its time have been the scene of terrible struggles, and blood shedding, as it dates from the days when Moors ruled in the North of Spain, and had to be wrested from the descendants of its builders only by many a tussle between the upholders of the Crescent and the Cross. On the inside of the city to the market place it has been modified, and Italianised, but to the thousands who pass up it daily from the lower parts of the outskirts, it wears its original Oriental aspect.

Ford gives to the word "Zocodover" quite another meaning and derivation. He explains it as "the square market." Whether he or Bermudez may be right, I know not, but, certain it is that either meaning may be aptly fitted to describe the spot to which our gateway leads—a spot of no comfortable memories—since it still reeks with the cruelties of genuine Spanish diversions, "Autos da Fe," and "Fiestas de Toros."

TOLEDO
EL TALLER DEL
MORO

PLATE XL.

TOLEDO.

INTERIOR OF THE "TALLER DEL MORO."

FROM the spring of the year 712, when Tarik, with his renegade
Jews and Berbers, wrested the city from its Gothic rulers, to the
spring of the year 1085, when Alfonzo VI.—the Emperor as he styled
himself after having won his laurels—reconquered the city for the
Christians, Toledo remained altogether an Oriental city, inhabited by
Berbers, strict Mahommedans and Jews, the last named being occasionally
tolerated and occasionally persecuted as they had been by the Goths, and
subsequently were by the Castilian Christians. The duration of this
tenure of power has to be borne in mind continually, in the endeavour to
assign dates to the Moorish monuments of this city, of which there are a
great number. It is of course true that long after the date of Alfonso's
conquest the Moorish artificers worked for the Christians, but such was
their constant condition of subjection that it is not to be credited that any
one of them could have been allowed to live in the wealth and luxury,
in which, whoever lived in the beautiful fragment of a Moorish house,
known as the " Taller del Moro," which forms the subject of the fortieth
sketch, must have lived. I can, therefore, have no hesitation in
repudiating for the date of its origin, as late a period as 1350, which

has been assigned to it. On the other hand, I am no less confident that Señor Escosura, who has written of it as 'of." between the ninth and tenth centuries," is also in error. What I believe is, that this elegant set of chambers was really one of the latest works in the city immediately preceding its capture by Alfonso, in 1085. The style of its work is certainly later than any of that executed under the Khalifate of Corduba while in the hands of the Ummeyàh family. It belongs, I believe, to the school of the Almohades, and reflects some of the novelties in complicated geometry introduced by the Arabs of Damascus, in advance of the Ummeyahs. They held to earlier types, as may be seen in all the works at Corduba, including even those ascribed to the author of the splendid Mih-ráb or sanctuary, the Sultan Al-Hakem II., who completed the "cubba," or Cupola of the Mih-ràb (the most complicated piece of design in all Cordova) in the year A.D., 965.

All that is left at present of this once sumptuous mansion consists of a central chamber, (fifty-four feet long by twenty-three feet wide), approached from a court-yard, the usual Moorish Alfagia, (no doubt, by the doorway shown on the right hand side of my sketch), and of two chambers, one at each end of the central one. Traces of colour and gilding have almost entirely disappeared, but the stucco ornamentation, where not wilfully or heedlessly destroyed, retains all its original sharpness and beauty. I found it in full use, or rather abuse, as a carpenter's workshop.

the "Taller del Moro"

TOLEDO
LA MAGDALENA

PLATE XLI.

TOLEDO.

TOWER OF THE CHURCH OF LA MAGDALENA.

*T*OLEDO is, or rather has been, a city of peculiar devotion. Its Christian mediæval architecture Mr. Street has fully illustrated, but he has passed hurriedly over some of the remains of that peculiar mixed style in which Christians usually gave the order, and Moors did the work. I have, accordingly, sketched two Christian-Moorish campaniles which he has not given, and one which he has, but from a different point of view.

The steeple of La Magdalena is, I fancy, of two periods, the construction from the ground to the base of the belfry being of one class, and the belfry itself of another. It has all the appearance of having been the old tower of a mosque previous to the conquest Toledo by King Alfonso, and of having been subsequently taken down to a certain level, and the belfry chamber and bells added, on the christianising of the structure.

It is built almost entirely of brick, and although simple to the extent of rudeness, its mass yet groups well with the long roof lines of the convents by which it is as it were hemmed in.

As the student wanders through these old streets of Toledo, rendered so picturesque by remnants of old Moorish use and ceremony, *attracted*

his mind is naturally ~~carried back~~ to the days when the " mezquita "
took the place of the church, and was thronged by the worshippers of
the " One God and Mahomet his Prophet," by day and by night.
The description given of the comparatively modern Moors in the
account of Commodore Stewart's embassy to the Emperor of Morocco,
in the year 1721, seems to carry us back to the days when
Toledo, and many other cities of Spain, owned ~~to~~ no other faith
than that defined by the Koran. " The Moors," says the writer,[*]
" seem not (as we do) to observe the day for business, and the night
for sleep, but sleep and wake often in the four-and-twenty hours, going
to church by night as well as day, for which purpose their Talbs
call from the top of the mosques, (or places of worship) having no
bells, every three hours throughout the city. In going to church they
observe no gravity, nor mind their dress ; but as soon as the Talb
begins to bellow from the steeple, the carpenter throws down his axe,
the shoemaker his awl, the tailor his shears, and away they all run like
so many fellows at football ; when they come into church, they repeat
the first chapter of the *Alcoran* standing, after which they look up, and
lift up their hands as much above their heads as they can, and as their
hands are leisurely coming down again, drop on their knees with their
faces towards the *Kebla*, (as they call it) or East and by South ; then
touching the ground with their foreheads twice, sit a little while on
their heels muttering a few words, and rise up again. This they repeat
two or three times, after which, looking on each shoulder, (I suppose
to their guardian angels) they say, *Selemo Alikem (i.e.,) Peace be with
you* ; and have done. When there are many at prayers together, you
wou'd think they were so many Gally-slaves a rowing, by the motion
they make on their knees."

TOLEDO

TOWER OF SAN
·PEDRO·MARTIRE·

PLATE XLII.

TOLEDO.

MOORISH TOWER OF SAN PEDRO MARTIRE.

PLATE Fourty-two presents us with another type of Christian-Moorish Campanile from that given by the last sketch. In this case the usual fashion of the mediæval church builders of dividing the total height of the tower into several compartments, pierced with largish openings on more than one floor, has been followed. The regular Arabian praying-tower is generally simply the inclosure of a staircase, with a gallery, or open chamber, only at the summit, from which " the faithful " are duly summoned by the Imaum to their devotions. The conversion of one or more stories into belfries, however, indicates (where the work is clearly that of a Mahommedan artificer), that he has been working only for the performance of the behests of a Christian, as in the case of the Tower of San Pedro Martire at Toledo. The Church itself exhibits only a clumsy and overgrown Palladian style of a thoroughly commonplace description, gloomy and uninteresting.

·TOLEDO·
S. TIAGO
DELA VEGA·

PLATE XLIII.

TOLEDO.

TOWER OF THE CHURCH OF SANTIAGO DE LA VEGA.

*T*HIS Church appeared to me to retain more of the primitive "Mezquita" or mosque than any other in Toledo, excepting the celebrated "Christo de la Luz." Its aspect is most picturesque as one descends from the city towards the Vega, or once rich and lovely plain. I could not help recognizing in it how good an effect might be produced in our ordinary street architecture by the use of common brick, provided that the masses of the construction should be artistically disposed, and used without the appearance of pinching here and paring off there, which spoils many of our usually too ambitious efforts.

In all such work as this in Spain, one is reminded only of the "bottom of the purse" when the work remains unfinished. With us the aspect of the "fond-du-sac" begins generally with the beginning, with the first lines of the disposition of the plan, and ends only with the end of the whole. As far as appearances go in this structure, differences of style from those of the rest of the building shown in my sketch in the belfry, and in the apsidal end of the choir of the Church, and in one or two other parts, seemed to point to those features of the design as being of considerably later date than that of the rest of the building.   If the primitive Moorish work may have been of the middle of the eleventh century, the Christiano-Moorish may have been of the end of the thirteenth.

TOLEDO
HOSPITAL OF THE
HOLY CROSS.

PLATE XLIV.

TOLEDO.

EXTERNAL VIEW OF THE HOSPITAL OF THE HOLY CROSS.

DESCENDING from the main Piazza of the city, through the gateway shown by the thirty-ninth sketch, the great " Hospedal de la Santa Cruz" is speedily reached. This is generally considered the finest example of Plateresque Architecture left in Spain, or probably ever erected in that country. Its founder was the all powerful Cardinal D. Pedro Gonzalez de Mendoza, " Tertius Rex," of Castile, Consolidator of the Monarchy, and Father of the absolute supremacy of the Catholic Church in Spain. The style of this building, and the circumstances of the birth and training of its architect, raise the important question of the extent to which the plateresque style in Spain may, or may not, have been of national origin? It appears that in 1459, a certain Anequin de Egas de Bruselas (or Brussels) of the Cathedral of Toledo, in his capacity of " Maestro Mayor" with his assistant Juan Fernandez de Liena, executed the façade of the main southern transept of that Cathedral, with the entrance familiarly known as "de los Leones." In this work, the architecture is of florid Burgundian-Gothic with scarcely a trace of Renaissance about its original design. Anequin died in 1494, and his son Henrique was appointed, by the Chapter of Toledo, to succeed his father as "Maestro Mayor," the duties of which office

he performed until his death in 1534. Henrique was the favourite
architect of the King D. Fernando, and of his son, the Archbishop
D. Alonzo, who actually disputed, in 1505, as to which of them should
for awhile avail themselves of his exclusive services. He was called
in to every important consultation of architects of his time, and was
evidently, " au courant " of the great changes of style which had been
developed in Italy, and which were in course of development in France,
and in and about his father's native place. His influence as a naturalizer
of the exotic details of which models were furnished to artists by the
prints of the "petits maitres," is clearly manifested when we recognise
the early dates at which his florid Renaissance buildings were executed.
For instance, in the two great works he designed for Cardinal Mendoza,
the dates of which are well known, we find Renaissance features
well carried out with scarcely any admixture of Gothic. The earliest of
these is the vast "Colegio Mayor" de Sta. Cruz at Valladolid, which
Henrique began in 1480 and completed in 1492, and the second the
splendid Hospital for Foundlings at Toledo, from which the sketch,
now under consideration, and the two which follow it have been taken.
In describing the second of these sketches, we shall resume our consideration of the Plateresque style generally from the point at which it is
now left. It may be well, however, with relation to this sketch, to
state that it shows the principal portal or great entrance to the Hospital,
and that the top story appears to be of later date, and coarser
execution, than the portal and the two elegant windows of the first
floor. The carving in the lunette of the doorway, represents, in very
good style, the "invention of the Cross" with Sta. Helena and the
Founder. The colour of the stone, and the quality of the workmanship leave nothing to be desired.

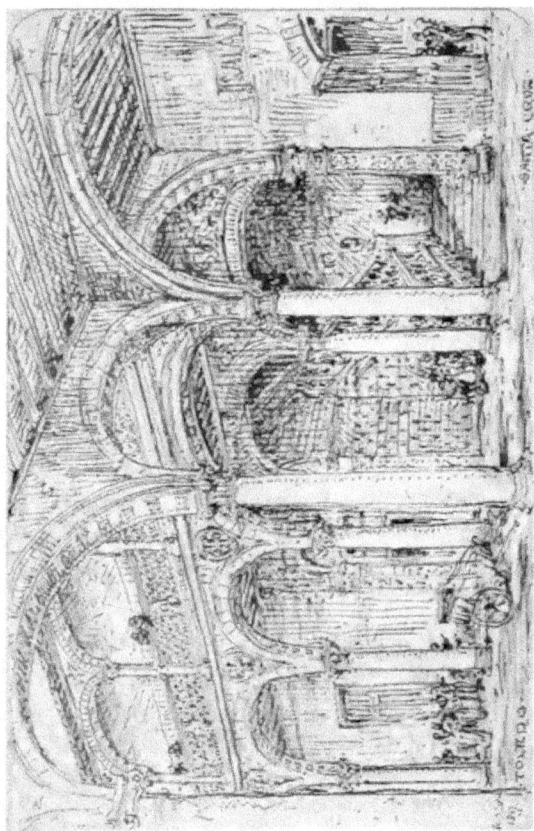

SANTA CROCE

TOLEDO

PLATE XLV.

TOLEDO.

CORTILE OF THE HOSPITAL OF THE HOLY CROSS.

I T is in the interior rather than on the exterior of the Toledo
Foundling Hospital, that Henrique de Egas has best shown his
command over the Plateresque style. It was no longer in the former a
question of adding on ornament in fanciful door and window dressings,
as it was in the latter, but a necessity to adopt or originate essential parts
of the structure, executing important functions of use and stability.
The columns, arches, and interspacing of the arcading of the Patios
evidence by their proportions, quite as much as by their details, that
Henrique's, and his employer's backs had been turned upon Gothic,
and that a new style had been inaugurated for Spanish architecture, as
the successes of Ferdinand and Isabella, and the discovery of America,
had laid the foundations of an entirely new era for Spain.

The construction of the building under notice, was begun by Cardinal
Mendoza, under Henrique, in 1504; the year in which those
Sovereigns ascended the throne, and completed in the year 1514.
Simultaneously, with the commencement of the great Hospital for
the " Tertius Rex," Henrique designed a still more extensive and
magnificent Hospital which the " Reyes Catolicos " proposed to

construct at Santiago, and entered upon many other great architectural works in other parts of Spain. Ford, who was no mean judge, says of the Hespedal de la Santa Cruz, that its " position overlooking the Tagus is glorious, and the building is one of the gems of the world; nor can any chasing of Cellini surpass the elegant Portal."

There is little doubt that Egas was stimulated to great exertion by the rivalry of many competitors, few of whom, however, designed in exactly his style. The work which most resembles his, I believe, will be found in the detail of the wonderful Plateresque Town Hall at Seville, and that of the Cathedral at Plasencia.

That so magnificent a Palace (for such it is) should have been thought necessary, or at any rate should have been indulged in, for the reception of foundlings, is to be partially accounted for by an old assertion I have met with, that the Spaniards, not knowing the parentage of the " niños perdidos," gave them " the benefit of the doubt," and considered them all as children of Hidalgos, a questionable compliment to the boasted morality, or any rate austerity, of the upper classes.

·TOLEDO·
HOSPITAL OF THE ·HOLY· CROSS.

PLATE XLVI.

TOLEDO.

DOORWAY FROM THE HOSPITAL OF THE HOLY CROSS.

THE fact that Moorish workmen should have been found in Toledo, Segovia, and elsewhere in Spain, to modify their national style, in their Mudejar work, and to incorporate freely in it many features of late mediæval work; while they scarcely ever lent themselves to any expression of Renaissance form, although they occasionally laboured in buildings of that style, has been supposed to imply a greater affinity between Arabian and Gothic modes of design, than between the Arabian style and Plateresque. This may, to some extent, account for the presence of this Mudejar work, assimilating in no way with the last-mentioned style, in a building of so distinctly Renaissance character as this one possesses. The fact is, however, rather thus—that after the expulsion of the Moors, and the institution of the Inquisition (the period of the construction of this Hospital), the Moorish artificers diminished very rapidly in number, and lost their individuality almost entirely, in Northern and Central Spain; and that, whereas, during several centuries they had lived there in cities in which Gothic architecture was practised by Christians, and had thus made themselves acquainted with its details, they had but a short term of scarcely tolerated national existence wherein to learn the novelties which were beginning to be taken up by the Spaniards, at the commencement of the sixteenth century.

My sketch, while it indicates the elaboration of this late specimen of Mudejar stucco-work, shows by the figures I have introduced (from life) the class to whose tender mercies this gem is now confided. Let it be hoped that the " Genius loci," may protect it, for the respectable Spanish soldier of the nineteenth century can scarcely be regarded as a satisfactory Conservative element.

TOLEDO
GREAT DOORWAY
OF THE
ALCAZAR

PLATE XLVII.

TOLEDO.

ENTRANCE GATEWAY TO THE ALCAZAR.

The Royal residence, for such is the meaning of the word "Alcazar," of Toledo, is one of the two great Palaces which Charles V. caused to be constructed in order that Spain might, for the first time, have "Royal Residences" commensurate with her grandeur and wealth. He appears to have chosen the same architect for both in the person of Alonso de Covarrubbias. This distinguished artist was born in 1527, at a locality in the diocese of Burgos, from whence he derived his name. At an early age, he allied himself with the family of the Flemish Egas, distinguished in the highest degree as architects in the persons of Anequin and his son Henrique. The wife of Alonso de Covarrubbias was a certain Maria Gutierrez de Egas, and by her he became the father of several sons, who in different ways (not in architecture) achieved great distinction and consideration. To return to the architectural career of Covarrubbias. Through the interest of Henrique de Egas, and probably in succession to him, Alonso Covarrubbias was appointed "Maestro Mayor" of the Cathedral of Toledo, whereupon he settled himself altogether in that city with his brother Marcos. His great work in Toledo Cathedral was the famous Chapel "de los Reyes nuevos," which he completed in the year 1534.

He is then said to have given some plans to Cardinal D. Alonso de Fonseca, for the improvement of the Archbishop's Palace at Alcala de Henares (see my notes on that Structure, Sketches, Nos. 33 and 34). He subsequently occupied himself, until 1537, in designing and carrying out the splendid entry to the Colegio Mayor (known as that of the Archbishop) in Salamanca, and other works.

In the last mentioned year he was appointed, by Charles V., with another architect, Luis de Vega, to make plans for rebuilding the Royal Palaces of Toledo and Madrid. This commission was subsequently modified, giving to Covarrubbias the works of Toledo, and to de Vega those at Madrid. The Alcazar of Toledo had been originally built by King Alonso VI, on the highest point of the city, when he took it from the Moors in 1085. It had been added to at various dates, chiefly by the powerful Alvaro de Luna, and lastly by the Reyes Catolicos. What Charles V. caused to be built, consisted of a façade of great extent, a magnificent vestibule, court-yard and staircase, upon which he placed his arms in many places. The Portal I have sketched, is stated by Cean Bermudez, from whom most of the above mentioned facts have been derived, to have been constructed by Henrique de Egas, under the direction of Covarrubbias who closed an honourable life, much favoured by his Sovereign, in 1570.

The Spaniards are justly proud of the noble simplicity, and grand style of Covarrubbias, which has none of the coldness and heaviness of Herrera's; and this is one of the rare cases in which they have made of late years, a really splendid and not over-loaded restoration. Upon the whole, the Alcazar at Toledo, is one of the few buildings existing in Spain which reflects, particularly in its grand Cortile, the "magnificenze" of the Italian Renaissance, in their completest form.

Probably a son of the more x?..... de Egas who died in 1534.

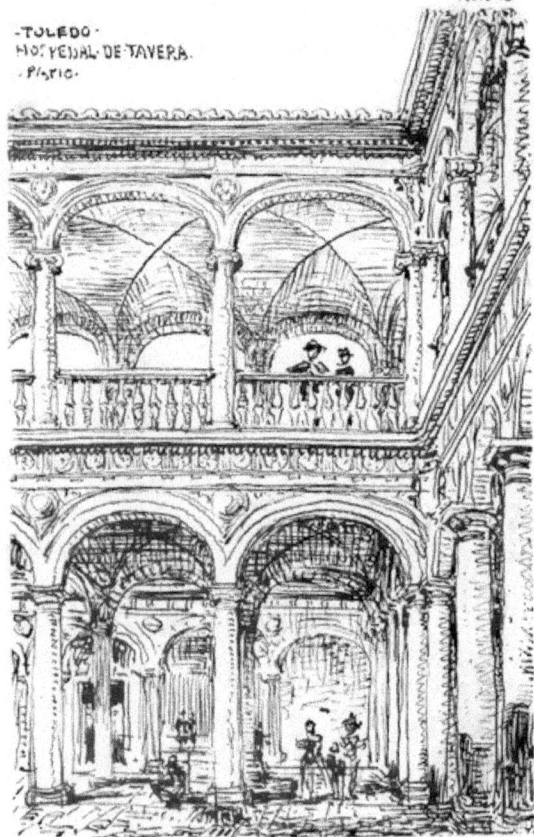

PLATE 48

·TOLEDO·
HOSPITAL·DE·TAVERA·
·PATIO·

PLATE XLVIII.

TOLEDO.

PATIO OF THE HOSPITAL OF CARDINAL TAVERA.

THE great Cardinal Primate, whose name this gigantic Hospital still bears was a worthy successor to Mendoza and Cisneros. In 1542 he employed the Architect Bartholomé de Bustamente to design and construct the four façades of this enormous pile. Not particularly attractive from without, internally the extent, fine proportions, and simplicity of its great Patios are very striking. It is one of the most regular pieces of Italian architecture I met with in Spain, and would have produced a highly satisfactory effect if its upper arches had been semi-circular instead of elliptic. The Hospital is dedicated to St. John the Baptist, and is placed without the walls of the city, whence its cognomen of "a fuera." The Church of the Hospital is older in style if not in date than the rest of the structure. Here in the room beneath the clock died the famous Berruguete in 1561, shortly after completing the portal of the Church and the marble monument within it which commemorates the cardinal virtues of the illustrious founder.

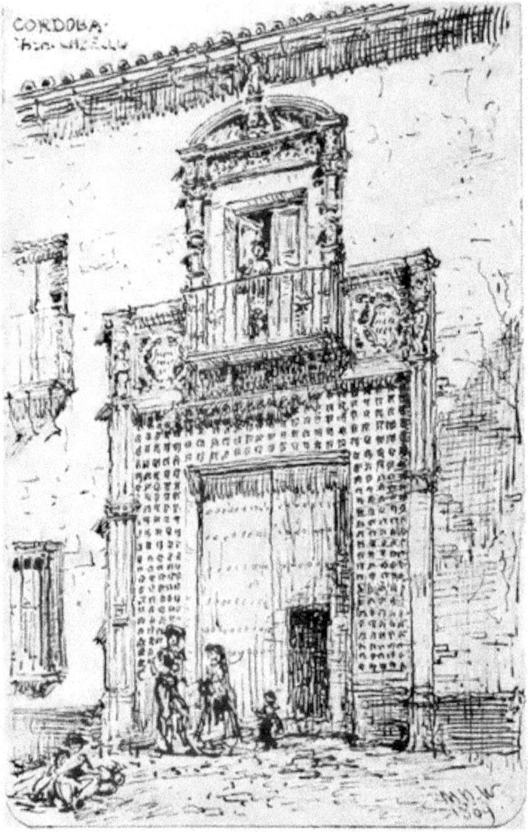

CORDOBA

PLATE XLIX.

CORDOBA.

EXTERIOR OF THE CASA CABELLO.

*T*HIS pretty entrance to a Spanish nobleman's house of the latter part of the sixteenth century has, like most of its class, mighty little story to tell, and that little, could I but unravel it, would probably turn out to be only of the dullest. Let us see, therefore, from a contemporary witness, what manner of life was ordinarily led by the class for one of whom it was no doubt fitted up in the fashion of the succeeding century. "In the morning as soon as they are up they drink water cooled with ice, and presently after chocolate. When dinner time is come, the master sits down to table; his wife and children eat upon the floor near the table; this is not done out of respect, as they tell me, but the women cannot sit upon a chair, they are not accustomed to it; and there are several ancient Spanish women who never sat upon one in their whole life. They make a light meal, for they eat little flesh; the best of their food are pigeons, pheasants, and their olios, which are excellent; but the greatest lord has not brought to his table above two pigeons, and some very bad ragoust, full of garlick and pepper; and after that some fennel and a little fruit. When this little dinner is over, every one in the house undress themselves an lie down upon their beds, upon which they lay Spanish leather-skins for coolness; at this time you shall not find a soul in the streets; the shops are shut, all the trade ceased, and it looks as if every body were dead. At two o'clock in the winter and at four in the summer they begin to dress themselves again, then eat sweetmeats, drink either some chocolate or water cooled in ice, and afterwards everybody goes where they think fit, and indeed they tarry out till eleven or twelve o'clock at night; I speak of people that live regularly; then the husband and wife go to bed, a great table-cloth is spread all over the bed, and each fastens it under their chin. The he and she-dwarfs serve up supper, which is as frugal as the dinner, for it is either a pheasant-hen made into a ragoust, or some pastry business, which burns their mouth it is so excessively peppered; the lady drinks her belly full of water, and the gentleman very sparingly of the wine; and when supper is ended each goes to sleep as well as they can."

PLATE L.

SEVILLE.

CHURCH OF LA FERIA.

" L A FERIA " in Seville, has been time out of mind the essence of all that is most " Picaresque " in the city. Not quite so thronged with Gitanos and Gitanas as the suburb of Triana, it makes up for shortcomings in that element of rascality and picturesqueness, by majos and majas, rustic beaux and belles, bull-fighters and beggars, dogs and donkeys, mules and muleteers, rags and tatters, and abundance of the most gloriously coloured fruits under the sun—and, above all, there reign such a sun and such a sky as denizens of the North have really little or no notion of. As if these elements of the picture were not enough, by way of background, stands a church in which the " battle of the Styles" seems to have been fairly fought out, with the victory now inclining to Moor, and now to Christian, while over all is seen a little of the Renaissance, with more than a suspicion in the heavy scrolls of the highest belfry, of " Churriguerismo."

While I sat on a door-step making this poor little sketch, I think I must have seen Murillos by the dozen, and John Phillips' by the hundred, not on canvas, but glowing with Nature's own light, and life, and colour.

PLATE LI.

SEVILLE.

CHURCH OF SAN MARCOS.

SOME notion of the richness of Seville, in the remains of old Moorish mosques converted into Christian churches, may be formed from the fact that this edifice, in which we find the two styles blended in the most interesting way, finds no mention in the pages of Ford, O'Shea, Mellado, or any other guide-books of Spain I have been able to meet with, except Bradshaw's. In that, Dr. Charnock thus briefly alludes to San Marcos. "Note," says he, "its beautiful western façade which has served as a model for several churches; the Retablo of the Altar de las Animas, contains a painting by D. Martinez; the tower rising to the left of the Church in imitation of the Giralda, is a fine monument of Arabian architecture." It is, of course, to the grand portal, rather to the whole façade, that Dr. Charnock alludes, since the former from the purity of its apparently late fifteenth century work, merits his praise, while the latter cannot certainly be regarded as other than a "barbarismo."

The tower is particularly pleasing in the style of its Mudejar additions, and has been engraved in elevation in ~~the great Government work~~, "los Monumentos Arquitectonicos." It is about seventy-five feet high by ten feet wide.

·SEVILLE·
·LA·FERIA·

PLATE LII.

SEVILLE.

REMAINS OF MUDEJAR HOUSE NEAR LA FERIA.

T HE habit of the Moors was almost universally to make their exterior architecture plain, and to reserve richness and elaboration for the interiors of their houses. The fact that what is commonly internal architecture has been used by Moorish workmen on the external façade of the little house which forms the subject of this fifty-second sketch would be sufficient of itself to prove that it had not been executed for a Moor, even if the Gothic mouldings and ornaments of the buttresses, imposts, cornices, and string courses failed to assert the Christianity of those for whom the house may have been built. The date of its construction, judging from style, was probably about the middle of the fifteenth century, at which period, in Spain, Renaissance features had in nowise affected the integrity of either Gothic or Moorish architecture. In this case all the mason's work is Gothic, and all the stucco-work is Moorish; and this distinction of style, according to the technical mode of construction, is not an uncommon feature of Mudejar work. It was not only in stucco-work that the traditions of Moorish art-workmanship enriched all Spain, since both in metal-work and wood-work they continued

to be employed long after their subjugation, preserving very many of ~~phase~~
their old and excellent types of form throughout many ~~epochs~~ of
transition.   To this subject I may have occasion to recur. I was
myself fortunate enough to meet with a beautiful little walnut-wood
box covered with Mudejar ornament, in the midst of which ~~the~~ a
Moorish workman had carved the I. H. S. of Christianity, and the
sword of Sant' Iago.

of the XVI century

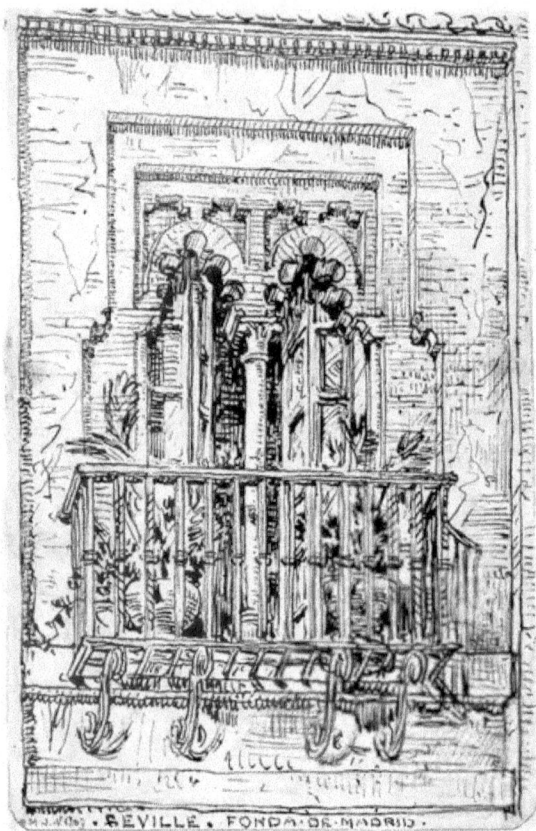

SEVILLE. FONDA DE MADRID.

PLATE LIII.

SEVILLE.

OLD WINDOW IN THE FONDA DE MADRID.

THIS window which is of the class known as " Ajimez," or literally "through which the sun shines," *i.e.* in an external wall, is a specimen of Mudejar work left "high- and -dry" as a "waif" in a part of Seville which, with this exception, has been entirely modernised. It belongs to exactly the house where one would least expect to find it, one of the best hotels, if not the best hotel, in Seville, the "Fonda de Madrid." All of this pretty window is made of brickwork, once covered apparently in Moorish fashion with thin plaster, excepting the column which is of white marble. The room it lights is an ordinary nineteenth century inn bedroom, with square casements, and not a vestige of the fifteenth century left about it. I could learn nothing about this relic, or perfect reproduction of the past, from my good host in the hotel, so that all I could do was to sketch it. While doing so, I could not but wonder how with so sensible, and, at the same time, pretty a window ready to their hands as a model, the builders of the Fonda could have been contented to execute the regular expressionless square-headed windows I found everywhere else. After a few minutes moralising in this vein, I began to ask myself whether, as an Englishman, I was not assiduously "plucking the mote from my brother's eye," with a beam all the time in my own

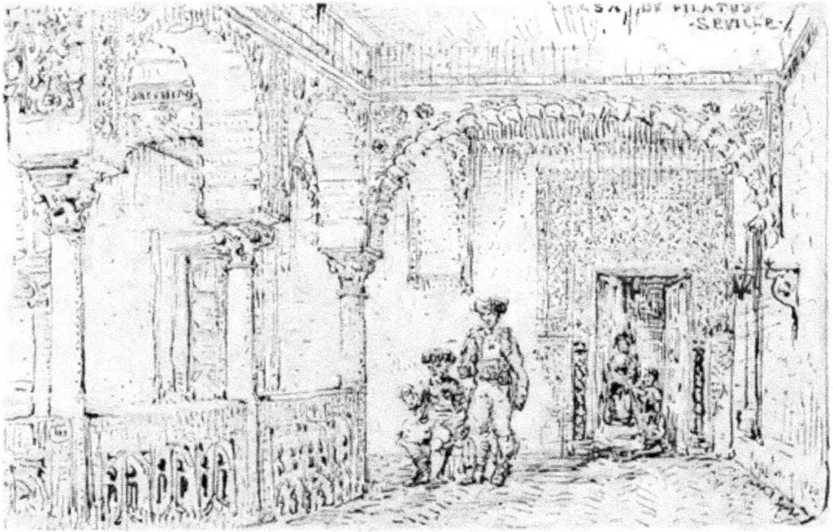
CASA DE PILATUS
SEVILLE

PLATE LIV.

SEVILLE.

VIEW IN THE UPPER STORY OF ONE OF THE PATIOS OF THE CASA DE PILATUS.

THE principal monument of Moorish magnificence still left in Seville, is, of course, the " Royal Residence," the " Alcazar," commenced in 1181, by Jalubi, the architect of Toledo. Next to it in importance is the " Casa de Pilatus," as it is called, from which this sketch, and the succeeding one have been taken. From the first named of these buildings I did not sketch at all, feeling myself entirely baffled by the extreme elaboration of all that was most interesting and admirable in the old Moorish, Mudejar and Plateresque work. Such a building can be in no wise now satisfactorily illustrated, excepting by one who may be in a position to devote much time and study to the task. " Restoration," and the adaptation of the structure to the necessities of nineteenth century life have so mystified the work and intention of the original designers, that although one may readily admire, it becomes exceedingly difficult to analyse, all that meets the eye. I have, therefore, preferred giving my attention, so far as this publication is concerned, to other, although less noteworthy, specimens of the domestic architecture of Seville.

The student of the Fine Arts, and even the ordinary traveller, are sure, without any urging on my part, to visit and enjoy the Alcazar, as a Royal Palace; but may possibly, and, indeed, unless advised on the subject, probably overlook the great beauty and curiosity of the old, and now sadly neglected, Moorish and cinque cento Garden which lies in the rear of the building. How to make a garden a delight the Mahommedans learnt from the Persians, and taught by example, if not by precept, to the Christians. Throughout these antique, orange, lemon, box, and myrtle, groves, the Moors carried their system of irrigation. Fountains and fishponds, baths and open water channels, even in the hottest summer, still cool the favourite haunts. Many of these, Pedro " el Cruel" caused to be formed in 1364 by architects specially brought from Granada to rebuild a large portion of the Palace, for his accommodation and that of his celebrated and beautiful mistress, Maria de Padilla. Much more modern, and far less beautiful, gardening was done by Charles V, but it is to the Moors the spot owes all its great charm.

To return to the " Casa de Pilatus," so called from an old tradition, that it was intended as a reproduction of the house of Pilate at Jerusalem. It was built in 1533, by Fadrique Henriquez de Ribera, after his return from a pilgrimage to Jerusalem in 1519. From him the Palace, for such it was, has descended (and, oh, how much descended!) to its present owner, who is said to rarely visit it, a Duke of Medina Cœli. From the Señor Duque, it has again *descended* to his Administrador, who does his best to keep it (for Spain) clean, and in tolerable order. My sketch has been taken in the upper gallery of the third Patio.

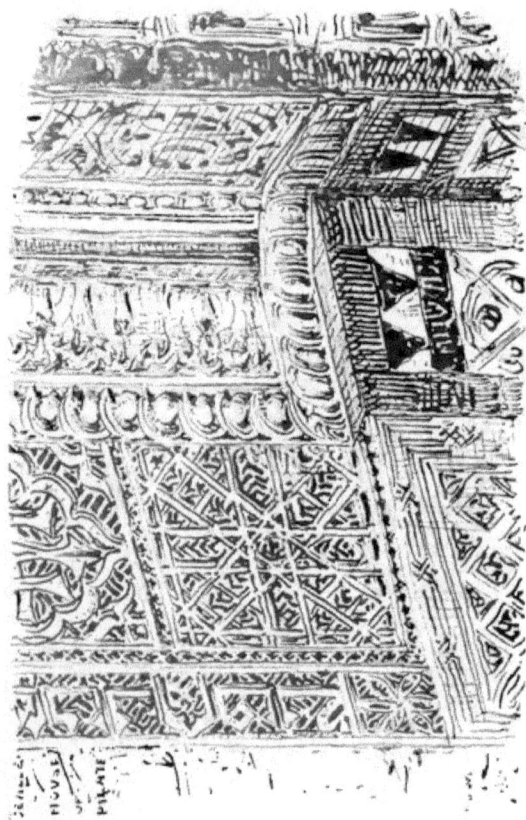

SEVILLE.

DETAIL FROM A DOORWAY IN THE UPPER FLOOR OF ONE OF THE PATIOS OF THE HOUSE OF PILATE.

THIS sketch represents, to a larger scale, a portion of the doorway shown upon a small scale in the preceding sketch. It illustrates two of the special points of architectural value in this fine old Palace, viz., the entirely Moresque character of the stucco-work at a comparatively late date, and the profuse use of " Azulejos" or coloured tiles. Some of these may be recognized, although in a sketch in black and white, it is not easy to make them apparent, in the coverings of the lower part of the door jamb. It is, however, in and about the splendid staircase, that this charming tile lining, of the use of which we have here of late years commenced a very satisfactory revival, asserts its value as a beautiful mode of introducing clean and permanent polychromatic decoration—the only mode, indeed, as I believe, suitable for our changeful climate, and smoky ways.

I regret that my sketch is not sufficiently minute to show a favourite habit of the Moors of Granada and Seville, in the technical working of their stucco, by the use of which they give an appearance of extraordinary elaboration to their decorations. It consists in working different patterns on different planes of the same piece of stucco-work. At a distance the dominant lines of the pattern only are apparent, on a nearer approach the pattern comes into sight which fills up the bold openings left between the dominant lines of the top pattern; and on a still closer inspection, a third series of forms running counter to the main lines of the pattern on the second plane and filling up the interstices of it may be traced. I am inclined to believe, from their peculiar sharpness, that few, or none, of the repeats of these patterns were done from moulds by the operation of casting, but that wire, or cut metal stencils, were used as guides for the pointed tools and knives, by which superfluous plaster was removed, whilst the whole was yet in a plastic state.

This method of shaping semi-plastic stucco with sharp tools, was, I have no doubt, derived by the Arabs from Roman tradition, as I have seen many examples of a similar mode of working at Rome Pompeii, Naples and elsewhere in Italy.

SEVILLE. CASA ALBA.

PLATE LVI.

SEVILLE.

ONE OF THE ARCHES OF THE PATIO OF THE CASA ALBA.

"HOW are the Mighty fallen," is the predominant sensation, as one wanders through these "banquet halls deserted." One may fairly paraphrase Byron, and declare that "in Seville Alba's echoes are no more." Ford and O'Shea, whose notes on the relics of domestic edifices in Spain are invaluable, both tell us that this still beautiful, though sadly destroyed, whitewashed, and dilapidated, old Palace, once "contained eleven patios, nine fountains, and one hundred marble columns." Of the elaboration of its workmanship, my sketch may serve to give some idea. It was probably next to the Alcazar, and the "Casa de Pilatus," the most important residence in the City. This house presents one of the rare instances in Spain, in which the Moorish stucco-workers have lent themselves to the rendering of Renaissance details. For these, no doubt, they were furnished with drawings or models, since in other parts of the same building, and especially in many beautiful rooms in the interior, where they have apparently been left to themselves, they have reverted partly to Mudejar work, and partly to the old types of geometrical enrichment, which may be regarded as

Repeated

specifically their own.   Much of this is almost reduced to a flat surface by ~~multitudes of~~ coats of whitewash.   I was very much pleased, however, to meet with one Spanish gentleman occupying a suite of rooms in the house, who was fully alive to the beauty of the Palace he lived in ; and who had, with his own hands, cleared off some of the whitewash, and restored much of the fine ornamental detail of his rooms to its original sharpness.   Would that there were more like him in Spain !

~~This house was formerly known as " de los Pinedos."~~

·SEVILLE·

·CASA· ALBA·

P/ATE LVII.

SEVILLE.

DETAIL FROM THE PATIO OF THE CASA ALBA.

*T*URNING from a consideration of the grand scale upon which the houses of the old Spanish nobility have been usually constructed, and the elaboration with which, as in the present sketch, the profuse ornamental detail has been combined with heraldic insignia to set forth the splendour and dignity of the family and its alliances, to the ruin and dilapidation which seem to have fallen alike upon the architecture and the families, one naturally wonders at the causes of the almost total wreck. Some may, no doubt, be found in active assailment from without, invasion, revolution, " y otras cosas de España;" but it is from within that the real main enemy—pride—has undermined all. During the latter part of the sixteenth, and early part of the seventeenth century, this national infirmity reached its acme. Witness emphatically the sketch given by an eye-witness towards the close of the last named century.

" It would grieve a body to see the ill-management of some great lords ; there are divers who will never go to their estates (for so they call their lands, their towns, and castles) but pass all their lives at Madrid, and trust all to a steward, who makes them believe what he

judges most for his own interest.   They will not so much as vouchsafe
to inquire whether he speaks true or false ; this would be too exact,
and by consequence below them.   This, methinks, is one considerable
fault ; the strange profusion of vessels only for an egg and a pigeon
is another.   But it is not only in these things which they fail, but it
is also in the daily expences of their houses.   They know not what it
is to lay up stores, or make provision of anything ; but every day they
fetch in what they want, and all upon trust, at the bakers, cooks,
butchers, and all other trades ; they are even ignorant what they set
down in their books, and they put down what price they will for every
thing they sell ; this matter is neither examined into nor contradicted.
There are often fifty horses in a stable, without either corn or straw,
and they perish with hunger.   And when the master is in bed, if he
should be taken ill in the night, he would be at a great loss, for they
let nothing remain in his house, neither wine nor water, charcoal nor
wax-candle, and in a word nothing at all ; for though they do not take
in provisions so near that there is nothing left, yet his servants have a
custom of carrying the overplus away to their own lodgings, and the
next day they furnish themselves with the same things again.   They
observe no better rules with the tradesmen.   A man or woman of
quality had rather die than to haggle for, or ask the price of a stuff,
or lace, or any other thing, or to take the remainder of a piece of
gold ; they rather chuse to give it the tradesman, for his pains of
having sold them for ten pistoles which was not worth five.   If there
is a reasonable price made, he that sells to them is so honest not to
take the advantage of their easiness to give whatever is asked them ;
and as they have credit given them for ten years together, without even
thinking of paying, so at last they find themselves under great difficulties
with their debts."

SEVILLE. M.C.W. 1857.

PLATE LVIII.

SEVILLE.

ARCHES FROM THE CASA DE LOS ABADES.

THE architectural style of this very pretty house, No. 9, in the Calle de los Abades, is much purer, that is more Italian, in its plateresque, than is usual in other houses in Seville in which the hand of the skilful Moorish operative is to be distinctly perceived. This is to be accounted for by the fact, that although the mansion existed as a house of importance at the commencement of the fifteenth century,* the architectural features which now meet the eye were all executed for the rich Genoese family of the Pinedos about 1533. If it were not for the peculiar engrailed double edging to the arches, the thinness of the marble central window shaft, and a few oriental turns here and there given to the foliage, and enrichments of the mouldings, one could almost believe that this architecture was regular Genoese cinque-cento. It is possible however, that although here in the midst of ordinary Spanish Plateresque one is tempted to cry out "Oh! how Italian this is!" if one could only meet with a precisely similar building in Genoa; one would be quite as much tempted to exclaim, "Oh! how Spanish

---

* O'Shea states (page 410) that the Infante Don Fernando, uncle of Juan II., lodged in it in 1407.

this is!" The fact of course is, that it exhibits a mixture of the two styles, produced under the exceptional circumstances to which I have alluded.

After passing from its Genoese owners, it was inhabited by certain Abades, rich members of the Cathedral Staff, who left behind them their name, but no very popular odour of sanctity,

> " En la calle de los Abades,
>   Todos han Tios, y ningunos Padres." *

So runs the jingle Ford quotes, with manifest glee, adding as a sequel to bring the matter home to the right offenders,

> " Los Canonigos Madre, no tienen nijos;
>   Los que tienen en casa, son sobrinicos." †

Possibly it may have been some of these very "sobrinicos" who hindered my sketching by many small practical "chistes," for as the Patio served as a play-ground to a tumultuous little boys' school, I found it by no means conducive to that state of mind which facilitates elaborate sketching. I fear also that such an occupation of its graceful galleries may not prove conducive to the preservation of the noses, and possibly even of the heads, of the "Caballeros de mucha consideraçion," who fill the medallions of the spandrels of the principal arches of the Patio.

* In the Street of the Abbots, all have *uncles* none *fathers.*

† The Cathedral Canons have no *sons,* those they keep at home are *little nephews.*

SEVILLE
CASA DE LOS ABADES

PLATE LI.

SEVILLE.

VIEW IN THE PATIO OF THE CASA DE LOS ABADES.

IN spite of all the habits of reckless extravagance in the days
when America poured its countless riches into the mother-
country described by travellers, and in spite of the quantity of money
which must have been lavished by nobles and superior ecclesiastics,
as in the case of the extremely elegant Renaissance "Casa de los
Abades," which forms the subject of our fifty-eighth sketch, the
home-life of Spain never approached the contemporary plenty and
comfort which obtained in Italy, France, and England. In spite
of the occasional prodigality of wedding feasts, such as that of
Camacho in Don Quixotte, and in spite, perhaps, of a little
occasional "gourmanderie" on the part of the "Senores Abades"
of this Calle, neither cooking nor service appear to have been
carried to much perfection. It is in fact very curious, in wandering
over any fine old Spanish house, to observe how little provision
appears to have been made in them architecturally for the kitchen
and its service. Ornament appears to have been much more general
in the public parts of the richest houses than good fare in the
interior and private parts. Nor was there any such movement

towards excess in this particular, as usually accompanies the passage
of a wealthy and powerful people from wealth and power, through
laziness, to poverty and weakness.

So late as 1775, the year in which Philip Thicknesse* travelled
through part of Spain, and whilst it was yet a comparatively
unbroken-up country, domestic luxury had reached but a little way
beyond the satisfaction of the simplest wants of nature in the
simplest way. "The people of fashion in general," he says, "have
no idea of serving their tables with elegance, or eating delicately ;
but rather, in the style of our forefathers, without spoon or fork,
they use their own fingers, and give drink from the glass of
others ; foul their napkins and cloaths exceedingly, and are served
at table by servants who are dirty, and often very offensive. I
was admitted, by accident, to a gentleman's house, of large fortune,
while they were at dinner ; there were seven persons at a round
table, too small for five ; two of the company were visitors ;
yet neither their dinner was so good, nor their manner of eating
it so delicate, as may be seen in the kitchen of a London
tradesman. The dessert (in a country where fruit is so fine and
so plenty) was only a large dish of the seeds of pomegranates,
which they eat with wine and sugar. In truth, Sir, an Englishman
who has been the least accustomed to eat at genteel tables, is,
of all other men, least qualified to travel into other kingdoms,
and particularly into Spain ; " especially, if what Swift says be
true, that a nice man is a man of dirty ideas."

* "A Year's Journey through France and Part of Spain," by Philip Thicknesse. Bath,
1777. Vol. I. pages 260-1.

·SEVILLE·

·A·PEEP·INTO·AN·ORDINARY·PATIO·

PLATE LX.

SEVILLE.

A PEEP INTO AN ORDINARY PATIO.

notices)

IN several previous ~~descriptions,~~ I have described the uses of the Patios in olden times, and on a large scale, and the degree to which they have been made, as architectural contrivances, to fall in with popular manners and customs. It remains to notice the extent to which the Spaniards of to-day sympathise in this respect with their forefathers, and how essential the Patio still is to the happiness of domestic life. It is at once cool and airy, and may be made quite private or semi-public at pleasure. With its iron gate to the street closed, and a screen drawn across it, it becomes private, and with its door opened it occupies in modern life exactly the position which the " Atrium " used to occupy in ancient classical life. An awning drawn across from side to side of the Patio answers to the Roman Velarium, closing the Impluvium ; and gives shade and softened light during the glare of mid-day, allowing the court of the house to be used as the ordinary sitting-room of the family. Theophile Gautier[1] gives a pretty picture of the facility with which the Patio may be converted at night into the " Salon," in which, what answers to the Soirée of the French, is usually given by the Spaniards. " The Tertullia," he says, " is held

* In his amusing " Tra los Montes." Bruxelles, 1843. Vol. II. page 44.

n the Patio which is surrounded by columns of alabaster, and ornamented with a fountain, the basin of which is encircled with flowers and masses of foliage, on the leaves of which the trickling drops fall in small showers. Six or eight lights are suspended against the walls, chairs and sofas of straw or cane furnish the arcades ; guitars are laid about here and there, and the piano occupies one angle and a whist-table another. The guests, on entering, salute the master and mistress of the house, who never fail, after the usual compliments, to offer a cup of chocolate, which may or may not be refused, and a cigarette which is generally accepted. These duties fulfilled, the visitor may attach himself to whichever group in the corners of the Patio he may consider most attractive. The family and the elderly guests play cards. The young gentlemen talk to the young ladies, and in fact, if they are so minded while away the time in innocent flirtation, or perhaps less innocent gossip and tittle-tattle." The Patio thus becomes the stage on which the elegant señoritas display their most winning fascinations, and " spin cobwebs to catch flies " in the shape of " novios."

It is principally in those cities in which classical and oriental tradition is still strongest, such as Segovia, Toledo, Granada, and Seville, that the use of the Patio, as the Romans and Moors used their open air Cortiles, is chiefly affected. Our sketch was taken in Seville, but hundreds of similar sketches might readily be taken there, or elsewhere. There is nevertheless a special charm about these Seville houses, in spite of their remorseless whitewash, which makes life in them most pleasant. This has no doubt justified the old proverb, quoted in German Latin and Italian by Berckenmeyern* " Wen Gott lieb hat, dem giebt er ein Haus in Sevilia." (To whom God loves he gives a house in Seville).

* Neu-vermehrter Curieuser Antiquarius. Hamburgh. 1731.

CADIZ. CATHEDRAL.

PLATE LXI.

CADIZ.

INTERNAL VIEW OF THE CATHEDRAL.

SWINBURNE,[*] who visited Cadiz in January, 1775, and who certainly possesses the merit (so far I can find out) of being the first Englishman who made any drawings from the remains of ancient architecture in Spain, found the Cathedral of that city, "la nueva," intended to supersede the mean "la vieja," built in 1597, in course of construction, and the following is his description of what he then saw. "On the shore stands the Cathedral, a work of great expense, but carried on with so little vigour, that it is difficult to guess at the term of years it will require to bring it to perfection; I think fifty have already elapsed since the first stone was laid, and the roof is not yet half finished. The vaults are executed with great solidity. The arches that spring from the clustered pilasters to support the roof of the church are very bold; the minute sculpture bestowed upon them seems superfluous, as all the effect will be lost from their great height, and from the shade that will

[*] Travels through Spain in the year 1775 and 1776, in which several monuments of Roman and Moorish architecture are illustrated by accurate drawings taken on the spot by Henry Swinburne, Esq. London. 4to. 1779.

be thrown upon them by the filling up of the interstices. From the sea, the present top of the church resembles the carcase of some huge monster cast upon its side, rearing its gigantic blanched ribs high above the buildings of the city. The outward casings are to be of white marble, the bars of the windows of bronze; but I fear the work will be coarsely done, if one may draw inference from the sample of a small chapel, where the squares are so loosely jointed and ill fitted, that in a few years the facing will be quite spoilt. It is unfair to prejudge a piece of architecture in such an imperfect state, but I apprehend the style of this will be crowded and heavy."

In spite of all Swinburne's forebodings the real effect of this Cathedral is now, internally at least, vast and stately, although in too florid a style as to detail to be quite satisfactory. The true cause of much of the delay, culminating in total stoppage in 1769, of which Swinburne complains, was the cupidity of certain Commissioners who appropriated to themselves the funds (a tax on American imports) allotted by the government for its execution. To give a cover to their gross dishonesty, they laid blame on the designs of the architect, Vicente Acera,* which could not, as they averred, be completed. At last, in 1832, the scandal was wiped out by the zeal and liberality of Bishop Domingo de Silos Moreas who caused the interior to be completed, and the exterior partially so, mainly out of his own privy purse.

* O'Shea adds the name of Cayon to that of Acera, describing the two as descending from the Salamanca school, founded by Churriguera and Tomé.

·MALAGA·

·THE·FOUNTAIN·OF·THE·ALAMEDA·

PLATE LXII.

MALAGA.

THE FOUNTAIN OF THE ALAMEDA.

IN almost every Spanish town there exists a feature, too often wanting, under similar circumstances, in England, in the shape of a public walk, or "paseo." In these popular airing places in the summer heats the inhabitants turn out, take exercise, meet and chat with one another, the poor with the rich (by mutual consent) under the shade of green trees, usually within compass of the scent of flowers, and almost invariably within hearing of the pleasant trickle of some pretty fountain. Such places, which, as their name imports, the Spaniards have inherited, with almost all that makes life pleasant, from the Moors, are called "Alamedas." In this particular Malaga is especially favoured, for not only is her Alameda, which forms the principle Plaza of the city, cooled by refreshing breezes from the sea,

> "La que baña dulce el mar
> Entre Jazmin y Azahar."

but it is adorned by one of the prettiest fountains in the world. It is made of pure white marble, and of such exquisite workmanship that it would betray its Italian origin at a glance, even if it did not possess a history of its own which places the fact beyond a doubt.

Ordered originally at Genoa by Charles V. for his Palace at Granada, it was shipped on its completion for conveyance thither on board a Spanish galleon.* On the voyage the vessel was captured by Barbarossa, and recovered by Don Bernardino de Mendoza, General de Galeras. Ford remarks that the costume (*à la* fig leaf) of the nymphs and Amorini which adorn it is somewhat too slight for Spanish ideas of propriety, and O'Shea caps his observation by commenting on its perfect suitability to the Malagan climate.

* There is a little discrepancy between Ford's and O'Shea's accounts, the former says that it was given by the Republic of Genoa to Charles V., the latter gives the facts as I have stated them.

MALAGA·
·GRAND·OLD·HOUSE·
·IN·THE·CALLE·SANT·AGUSTIN·

PLATE LIII. _X_

MALAGA.

RENAISSANCE HOUSE IN THE CALLE SANT AUGUSTIN.

NOT only is Malaga endowed with an "eternal summer" by its lovely climate, there being actually no "winter of its discontent," but it has also enjoyed historically a splendid and long summer of prosperity, its present state being comparatively ~~a twilight~~. _Autumn_ This "golden age" existed under the Moors for many centuries preceding the dreadful siege laid to the city by the Catholic kings, which ended on the 18th of August, 1487. It has never altogether recovered from the christianising influences then brought to bear upon it, though the charms of its position and climate prevented its being altogether deserted at any time. They indeed produced an after-crop of splendour, in the shape of fine residences of powerful nobility, enriched many of them by the spoils of the Moors, and yet more by the silver of America and the great profits of the foreign trade, to say nothing of the smuggling carried on in its port. Of such our sketch presents a specimen, more Italian in its character than would be likely to be met with in Spain, in any other locality than a "Port de Mer." The great establishment of the Genoese merchants, the "Casa de los Genoveses," may have exercised a powerful local influence upon the arts, and especially the architecture of Malaga, as that of our " Merchants of the Steleyard " did upon those of London.

In the distance is seen one of the cupola-covered towers of the vast Cathedral—most promising and picturesque from a distance, but unsatisfactory in its incompleteness, when visited by the Ecclesiologist.

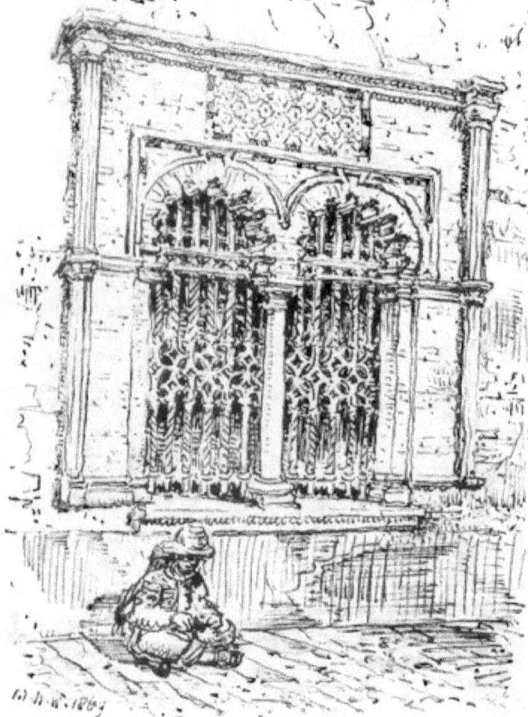

PLATE 64

MALAGA. OSPEDALE DE SANTO TOMÉ.

PLATE LIV. X

MALAGA.

OLD WINDOW OF THE OSPEDALE DE SANTO TOMÉ.

THIS pretty window of, as I believe, the early part of the sixteenth century is evidently of Mudejar design with little of the Moorish element left in it, excepting the obvious Orientalism of the workman. Take away the engrailed intrados of the arch, and the little dove-tailed break in the line of the archivolt, and all that is Moorish in the design would disappear; but still the particular mode of combining the brick and tile work would be left to show the disinclination of the Moor to quit or alter his old technical habits as an operative.

This window is associated in my memory with some sad scenes of suffering. It is situated, as it were, on the road to a sort of wicket or buttery-hatch, at which aid is given daily to cripples out of the funds of the great Hospital of Santo Tomé. At an early hour these poor creatures, the halt, maimed, diseased, and blind, take up their stations against the wall, and gradually creep onwards towards the spot at which the distribution takes place. The " Ay de mis " and " Por l'amor de Dios," echo in a dismal strain, interrupted only by a few especially ferocious oaths as one a little stronger or more active than the rest struggles forwards to cheat the others of their turn. The whole scene would have made an admirable subject for Callot's needle, Hurtado de Mendoza's pen, or Van Obstal's chisel. Lazarillo de Tormes and his blind "Amo" sat before me ; and one could clearly recognise what it must have cost noblemen, like D. Miguel de Manana and his "cofrades" of the vast Hospital of the "Caridad" at Seville (the prototype no doubt of the Malagan Hospital), to carry on their works of mercy in the midst of a dirt and squalor which should be seen to be realised.

MALAGA. DOOR OF SANTIAGO.

PLATE LXV.

MALAGA.

KNOCKER OF THE MONASTERY OF SANT' JAGO.

TRAVELLERS in Spain rarely fail to observe and comment on the great strength of the entrance doors, the thick planks forming which are frequently held together by iron bars, or plating, with ponderous bolts, or nail-heads, often of very pretty design. Such doors have descended apparently from Roman days, and the retention of the type, by Moor and Christian down to the present day, has been regarded as an evidence of the proverbially jealous temperament of the Spaniard. I think it bears a much clearer testimony to the want of good police in the streets, and the frequency of quarrels and rows, to say nothing of marauders and more serious fighters in disastrous times. One is strengthened in this belief by the inclination ever shown by the old Spaniards to have as few external windows as possible on the ground floors of their houses, and those few raised high above the pathway, and protected by close and strong iron grilles and thick shutters. These may have been useful restraints on the love-making propensities of the Spanish Lotharios; but the difficulties they presented to pilferers and "Soldados de Fortuna," when a little out of luck, were, perhaps, of even greater importance to the householder.

The portion of the door I have sketched, formed part of a solid defence against a formidable class in Spain, bold in attack, and not easily cast down even in retreat—the beggars.   Much of the enormous sums given by the devout to God in Catholic times, this class believed they had as good right to scramble for as the monks; and it behoved the latter to fortify themselves, as they never failed to do, pretty strongly against the importunity of the former.   No doubt the coronetted knocker of the Monastery of Sant' Jago was intended to inspire the beggars with fitting awe, and an intimation that it was not to be audaciously handled by vulgarity.   Some such scarecrow was certainly locally necessary, for I well remember being driven away by clustering beggars no less than four times before I could accomplish my very hasty sixty-fifth sketch.

PLATE LXVI.

GRANADA.

REMAINS OF THE ALHAMBRA AS SEEN FROM THE ALBAYCIN.

NO one looking from the quarter of the city to which, after its conquest by the Christians in 1480, the Moors who lingered behind the bulk of their fellows, were relegated (as the Jews by the Popes to the Ghetto at Rome) would be justified in supposing that the stern-looking and dilapidated fortresses, and lines of walling of vast height and apparent strength, which meet the eye, contained nearly complete specimens of the loveliest and most elaborate system of ornamentation, both in form and colour, which has ever existed. The position of the Alhambra is worthy in every respect of the treasures of art it contains. It overlooks the Vega, an extended plain, which in the days of the city's prosperity was literally one vast garden, and even in the present day is, to most of central Spain, pretty nearly what an oasis may be supposed to be to a desert.

On the extreme left in this sketch is seen the great mass of the "Torre de Comares," which contains the celebrated Hall of the Ambassadors; next to it on the right are the ancient buildings of the Patio de la Mezquita or Mosque. Behind these, and further to the right, rises the great rectangular mass of the Palace of Charles V. The flat space, in front and on the right of the Palace, is known as the Plaza de los " Algibes " (of the tanks) and the mass of towers and buildings beyond are those of the Alcazaba, (the fortress) with, conspicuous on the extreme right, the Torre de la Vela, the Watch-Tower, from which a constant look-out was kept far and wide over the city to the west, and the far spreading Vega to the west and south. On the horizon stretched the great range of snow-clad mountains, the Sierra Nevada.

The beauty of the view from this tower cannot be exceeded, and I never shall forget the aspect of the scene upon one especially lovely moonlight night. By such soft illumination, the desolation of which one sees so much by day is passed over in the breadth of the great masses of light and shade. As the moonlight caught the snow-clad peaks of the Sierra Nevada, and traced itself in the silver lines of the winding River Genil, until coming from the far off distance to the city beneath, in the thousands of twinkling lights of which its silver threads got tangled and lost, everything seemed perfect; and as one turned away towards the nearer mountain heights, and saw upon their hilly eastern slopes the Generalife, and the Alhambra, almost close at hand, one felt inclined to forget the present in the past and to think of ruin as perfection, and of death as life.

By day the illusion was destroyed, the young Alhambra of the night faded away, and in its place one saw all the seams and stains and wrinkles age had left upon its hoary head and face, all the more painfully perhaps from the efforts one recognises as having been made here and there, by loving and anxious hands, to mend and palliate conspicuous decay.

GRANADA

ENTRANCE TO THE BOSQUE DEL ALHAMBRA

PLATE LXVII.

GRANADA.

ENTRANCE TO THE BOSQUE DEL ALHAMBRA.

OUR sixty-seventh sketch illustrates the road by which the traveller usually ascends from the City of Granada to the delights of the Alhambra. On passing through the massive gateway, seen in the middle of the sketch, he finds himself in a thickly-planted wood or "bosqué," cool, shady, refreshing, and beautiful. At several turns in the winding road, fountains, abundantly supplied with crystal water, charm his eye and ear at the same moment. With his pulse just quickened by the gradual ascent, everything seems to conduce to ease of body, and to throw him into a happy frame of mind for enjoying the feast of beauty which lies in store for him. As a preparation for such a banquet, I know nothing better calculated to insure a healthy digestion of the artistic "pabulum" the Alhambra furnishes, than a thorough acquaintance with the views of Owen Jones upon the subject of Moorish art generally.

If in his noble work on the Alhambra he has described the system of decoration of the Moors, it is in his "Grammar of Ornament" that he has weighed its sterling metal, against all the various alloys which have in history, at different times, been more or less confounded with it.   For instance as compared with Arabian Art the following is his verdict: "Generally, the main differences that exist between the Arabian and Moresque styles may be summed up thus, the constructive features of the Arabs possess more grandeur, and those of the Moors more refinement and elegance."*

The art of the Turks he places on a lower platform than that of the Arab, and therefore far below the Moorish. Their system of ornamentation he says "Is a modification of the Arabian, bearing about the same relation to this style as Elizabethan does to Italian Renaissance.

"When the art of one people is adopted by another having the same religion, but differing in natural character and instincts, we should expect to find a deficiency in all those qualities in which the borrowing people are inferior to their predecessors.   And thus it is with the Art of the Turks as compared with the Art of the Arabs: there is the same difference in the amount of elegance and refinement in the Art of the two people as exists in their national character." While he acknowledges the extent to which Arabian, and consequently Moorish Art may have been originally indebted to Persian, he considers that the former ever maintained a superiority over the latter. This he accounts for by observing that, "the Persians, unlike the Arabs and the Moors, were free to introduce animal life, and this mixing

* A comparatively new light has been thrown upon the refinement of Arabian work by the exquisite illustrations contained in the fine work, "L'Art Arabe," by M. Prisse d'Avennes. Paris, 1871. Motel.

up of subjects drawn from real life in their decoration led to a much
less pure style of ornament. With the Arabs and Moors, ornaments
with their inscriptions had to supply every want, and reached a
higher point of elaboration. Persian ornament is a mixed style:
combining the conventional, which is similar to the Arabian, and
probably derived from a common origin, with an attempt at the
natural which sometimes has influenced both the Arabian and Turkish
styles, and is even felt in portions of the Alhambra. The great
attention paid to the illuminating of manuscripts in Persia, which,
doubtless, were widely disseminated in Mohammedan countries, would
readily spread the influence of this mixed style. The decorations of
the houses of Cairo and Damascus, the mosques and fountains of
Constantinople, more especially, exhibit this mixed style; groups of
natural flowers are constantly found growing from a vase and enclosed
in panels of conventional Arabian ornament. The ornament of modern
India also feels this ever present influence of the Persian mixed
style." These words are not, it should be remembered, those of a
casual observer, of a traveller who records the fleeting impression of
the hour, but of the man who better, I believe, than any other
living man understands the subject upon which he is speaking. His
knowledge too is not that of the theorist only; as a practical designer
he has tested the applicability of the lessons he has derived from his
studies, and shown that such studies lead to certain and foreknown
results of great beauty, applicable to the Arts and Industries of the
Present, as he traced their perfect harmony in days of old with the
Arts and Industries of the Past.

Of the Alhambra itself as the culminating point of Moorish Art,
as the Parthenon is of Greek Art, he declares his belief that there is

" no work so fitted to illustrate a grammar of ornament as that in
which every ornament contains a grammar in itself. Every principle
which we can derive from the study of the ornamental art of any
other people is not only ever present here, but was by the Moors
universally and truly obeyed."

" We find in the Alhambra the speaking art of the Egyptians, the
natural grace and refinement of the Greeks, the geometrical combinations of the Romans, the Byzantines, and the Arabs. The ornament
wanted but one charm, which was the peculiar feature of the Egyptian
ornament, symbolism. This the religion of the Moors forbade; but
the want was more than supplied by the inscriptions, which, addressing
themselves to the eye by their outward beauty, at once excited the
intellect by the difficulties of deciphering their curious and complex
involutions, and delighted the imagination when read, by the beauty
of the sentiments they expressed and the music of their composition.
To the artist and those provided with a mind to estimate the value of
the beauty to which they gave a life, they repeated *Look and Learn*."

It is not, of course, from the study of the monuments of one
period, or of one locality, that any accurate idea is to be formed of
the Architecture of any races, whose national history and whose
dominion have extended for many centuries over many lands. Nor,
indeed, is a just appreciation of the artistic value of the system of
Art, sectionally studied, to be arrived at until the student has compared
it with its antecedents in its own and other localities. Such works,
therefore, as offer to the inquirer means for instituting studies of the
nature alluded to, acquire peculiar value, although necessarily incomplete
for sectional study. The student of Oriental Architecture, from this
point of view, has been laid under a debt of gratitude by M. Girault

de Prangey,[*] whose works enable him to obtain a fair idea of the varieties of style practised by the Mahomedan races in Asia Minor, Syria, Egypt, Spain, Sicily and Barbary. Through all these there evidently runs a harmony of system, but not the less clearly have we to recognize an endless variety of detail, and an incessantly changeful development—reaching its climax certainly in the Alhambra at Granada.

[*] See especially for Spain, his "Monuments Arabes et Moresques de Cordoue, Séville et Grenade," Paris, 1832-3, and its continuation—"Monuments Arabes d'Egypte de Syrie et d'Asie Mineure," 1842-5, Paris. The above are essentially pictorial works, but in his "Essai sur l'Architecture des Arabes et des Maures," &c., Paris, 1841, he has discussed the whole subject historically with much ability.

GRANADA · PUERTA DE JUSTICIA ·

PLATE LXVIII.

GRANADA.

PUERTA DE JUSTICIA.

WENDING his way upwards through the beautiful " Bosqué," it is on arriving at the celebrated "Gate of Justice "* that the traveller first finds himself face to face with the Moor, and his wise and patriarchal habits, as well as his inherent love for the beautiful. Within these venerable walls once sat the Monarch, as Solomon sat, to administer justice to the poorest, as to the richest, of his subjects. On the side shown to the outer world the archway wears the stern features of the fortress, while on the inner side, the one shown in my sketch, there are traces of a beauty and richness suitable to the Palace to which it led. What is most remarkable architecturally about this Gateway is, firstly, the ingenuity of its plan for resisting surprise in attack; and, secondly, the beauty of the coloured tiles by which its inside elevation is decorated.

First, with respect to its plan. This, so far as the passage way from gate to gate (carried between walls of great thickness and massive construction) is concerned, assumes the form of two letters L

---

* Plan section and elevation of the outer side of this Gateway, to a large scale, will be found on Plate II. of Owen Jones's great work on the Alhambra. I sketched the interior of this Gateway, mainly because that was the only part of it he had not given.

placed in contact with one another, thus, ˌ▭˒, the gate of entry from without being at A, and the gate of exit at B. The consequence is that no assailant entering from A can form any idea of what preparations for resistance may exist in the interior of the gateway. Neither can he gain anything by a rush, as the impetus of any attack would be broken by the necessities of having to stop, turn round and start in another direction for too short a distance, before having to check and turn again, to acquire any momentum or "élan." Even after fighting his way from gate to gate, the assailant would only find himself in a narrow gallery between high walls and upper platforms through which it would be most difficult to advance, exposed to missiles from every direction. While attacking the outer gate and intermediate obstacles, the besieger would, of course, be liable to the amenities of molten lead, &c., from the upper chambers of the Gateway.

Secondly, with respect to the beauty of the coloured tiles. These are unlike, both in colour and texture, as well as I could see, any other tiles existing in the Alhambra, or any left at Cordova, Seville or Toledo. My impression is, that they may have been a present from Damascus, Cairo, or from Persia proper. The peculiar deep granulated blue which is conspicuous in them, I have only seen in fragments of ancient Mosques which have been brought from the East. The mode of manufacture is not that either of the usual Moorish and Spanish Azulejos, with raised outlines forming compartments for the separate colours; nor is it like that of the Majorca tiles and dishes, and the usual flat tiles of the Alhambra, which, with their fine white surfaces for painting on, formed the basis of Majolica. It is, however, quite like that of the half-encaustic, half-painted tiles of the early Mahommedan buildings in India, Persia, and especially Arabia proper.

A long inscription occurs in two lines over the inner gateway, towards the exterior. The following is from the translation of the distinguished Arabic student and historian, Don Pasqual de Gayangos.

" This gate, called Bábu-sh-shari'ah (the Gate of the Law)—may God prosper through it the law of Islám, and He made this a lasting monument of His glory—was built at the command of our Lord, the Commander of the Moslems, the warlike and just Sultan Abú-l-walíd Ibn Naor, (may God remunerate his good deeds in the observance of religion, and accept of his valorous performances in support of the faith). And it was closed for the first time in the glorious month of the birth of our Prophet, in the year 749. May the Almighty make this gate a protecting bulwark, and write down its erection among the imperishable actions of the Just."

THE ALHAMBRA ·
SALA DE LOS EMBAJADORES

PLATE LXIX.

GRANADA. THE ALHAMBRA.

SALA DE EMBAJADORES.

TO describe the progress of the visitor through the Courts and
apartments of the "Casa Real," as the Palace of the Alhambra
is called, would be to echo a more than thrice-told tale. For present
purposes, it may suffice to say, that in the Hall of the Ambassadors
he reaches the acmé of Moorish magnificence. My sketch represents
one of the nine windows by which the hall is lighted on the level of
the floor. The space from the single arch, which is on the internal
face of the apartment, to the coupled arches which are on the external
face of the building, represents the thickness, no less than about eight
feet, of the wall of the Tower of Comares. The window I have chosen
for sketching, looks towards a Renaissance addition to the Alhambra,
made by Charles V. for the accommodation of his Queen.

This elegant pavilion, from which is obtained a view of almost
unparallelled loveliness over the Vega, is known as the "Tocador de
la Reina," or, Boudoir of the Queen.

The Hall of Ambassadors occupies the whole of the internal area
on plan of the Tower, and is an apartment thirty-seven feet square
and seventy-five feet high. It is entered from the Court of the

" Blessing," as Mr. O'Shea considers the Patio de la Berkâh to be more properly called, than the Court of the Fish Pond, or " de la Alberca," the title by which it is usually known. Advancing from the Patio, the visitor traverses the Sala. Opposite to the door of entrance to the Hall are three windows, almost precisely like them I now give. In the central one appears to have been placed the throne of the Sultan. In each of the walls, on the right and left of the entrance, are three nearly-similar windows: the one I have selected for representation being the middle one of the three in the wall on the right upon entering. The dado which runs round the whole of the splendid Hall, is made of Mosaic and Azulejos for a height of about four feet from the pavement; and above it run bands with inscriptions and medallions. Over these, the walls, covered with lace-like diapers in stucco, to a height of about seven and twenty feet from the floor, run up to a second tier of windows, five on a side, lighting the upper portion of the Hall. At a height of about forty feet, occurs a beautiful stalactite cornice from which starts a noble dome, or " Artesonado" ceiling, most ingeniously made in inlaid wood, gorgeously (and) most harmoniously decorated. This ceiling, splendid as it is, occupies the place only of one yet more marvellous, which fell down. The original ceiling, or rather hollow cone, was of the same description as the existing stalactite, or pendentive, ceilings of the Hall of " the Abencerrages," of " Justice" and of " the two Sisters;" but larger and finer. Mr. Owen Jones has given us, in Plate VII of his magnificent work, a long section, to a large scale, passing from the window in which the throne of the Sultan was placed, through the Hall of the Ambassadors with its arch of entrance, through the Sala de la Barca, the splendid anteroom, as it were, to the Throne room, through the Loggia, or Arcade, of the Patio of the Alberca, through the Patio itself, and through the end Loggia of the Court with its exquisite Pavilion on the first floor. From this section can be admirably realised, what must have been the view, or "colpo d'occhio," of the Sultan, as he sat upon his throne to receive foreign Ambassadors.[*] It seems impossible to conceive of any position more imposing, or better calculated to impress the imagination particularly of Eastern magnates. Even now, bereft of so much that must once have added immensely to its charm, the view is one of exquisite and most romantic beauty. It is, indeed, a sight to stir a poet's heart, although

> "Lonely and still are now thy marble halls,
>   Thou fair Alhambra! there the feast is o'er;
> And with the murmur of thy fountain falls,[†]
>   Blend the wild tones of minstrelsy no more.
> Hushed are the voices, that in years gone by,
>   Have mourn'd, exulted, menaced, through thy towers,
> Within thy pillar'd courts the grass waves high,
>   And all uncultured bloom thy fairy bowers.
> Unheeded there the flowering myrtle blows,
>   Through tall arcades unmark'd the sunbeam smiles,
> And many a tint of soften'd brilliance throws
>   O'er fretted walls and shining peristyles."[‡]

---

[*] A pretty coloured view from this very point will be found in M. Girault de Prangey's "Choix d'Ornements moresques de l'Alhambra," Paris, 18—. Plate No. 3.

[†] It is believed that an alabaster fountain once occupied the centre of the Sala de Embajadores.

[‡] It is but just to Señor Contreras to remark that the Poet's picture was sketched before the date of his admirable conservatorship. He is a true artist, and has done wonders in the way of restoration, completing and as little as possible interfering with the marvellous picturesque character of the noble old Palace.

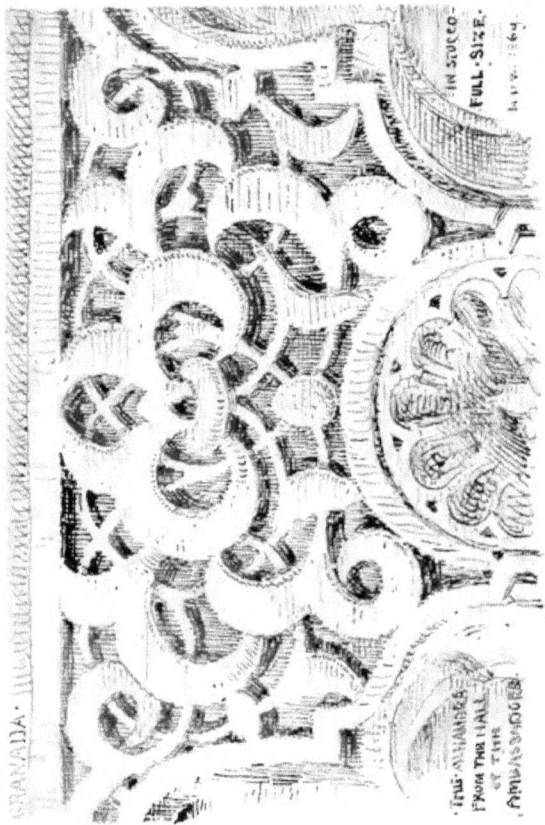

GRANADA. ILLUSTRATED BORDER OF PANEL

IN STUCCO.
FULL SIZE.
NOV. 1869.

THE ALHAMBRA
FROM THE HALL
OF THE
AMBASSADORS.

PLATE LXX.

GRANADA.—THE A͟L͟HAMBRA.

STUCCO DETAIL FROM THE HALL OF THE AMBASSADORS.

*I*N describing the subject of the last sketch, our theme was the general aspect of the "Sala de los Embajadores." I have chosen to let this minute specimen of its detail follow the statement of its large dimensions, in order the more forcibly to convey an idea of its wonderful elaboration. The elegant morsel of stucco-work now presented to the student has been actually traced from a portion of the stucco-work of one of the window recesses immediately above the dado. It affords an admirable illustration of two principles constantly followed by the Moors in their treatment of decoration—viz., to preserve the continuity of all scroll work from root to fully developed foliation—a principle entirely disregarded in all previous ornamentation based upon classical practice— and to care first for larger surfaces to satisfy the eye with harmonious relations of those surfaces to one another, and to the spaces they have to enrich, from a distance; and then to provide minor fillings and intersections so as to supply adequate elaboration for close inspection. In addition to the decorative effect

produced by variations in relief, still greater refinement was obtained
by patterns in colour, painted upon the surfaces of the modelled
ornaments. Although almost everywhere the colour has either been
rubbed off, or rubbed into confusion, the abrasion has affected for the
most part only the pigment and its albuminous vehicle, leaving the
surface of the stucco bare, and showing the outline of the delicate
ornament which has been drawn in by the pencil of the artist.

It is on the nature of the stucco itself I think it may be well to
offer here a few remarks. It certainly appears to be harder, closer in
texture, tougher, and much less absorbent, than gypsum or plaster of
Paris, when set in the usual manner. Lime alone, as ordinarily slacked,
would not I believe give any such texture, even if it could be
manipulated into similar ornamental forms. I believe the Moorish
Stucco to be almost if not quite identical with the Indian "Chunam,"
and that in its turn to be a substance produced much in the same
way that the fine Stucco of the Romans was ordinarily wrought by that
people. In the treatment of all of these substances, I believe four
peculiarities to have been generally used in common. Firstly—to
employ the finest lime only. Secondly—to mix it with pounded earthen
ware. Thirdly—to beat it thoroughly. Fourthly—to use saccharine
substances to retard the setting and keep the mass plastic under
the tool.

The present is scarcely a fitting occasion upon which to state in
any detail the ground upon which I have been led to this conclusion,
but I have little doubt that any student will be struck by the identity
of practice of Roman, Indian, and Moor, who will refer to the
practical descriptions of the various modes of the formation of terraces
given by Vitruvius, by Captain Phipps, in "The Barrackmaster's

Assistant,"* and by John Windus, in his "Journey to Mequinez."†

I have elsewhere noticed the command the descendants of the Moors seemed to retain over all operations of plaster and lime work throughout Spain, as evidenced by the beauty and elaboration of the Mudejar style in those materials, long after they ceased to be the dominant race in the localities in which they continued to practice their old technical arts.

* Calcutta, 1811.

† "A Journey to Mequinez, the residence of the present Emperor of Fez and Morocco, on the occasion of Commodore Stewart's Embassy thither for the redemption of the British Captives in the year 1721." London, Jacob Tonson. 1725. A very interesting old book, the descriptions in which carry the mind forcibly back to the Moorish occupation of Spain.

THE·ALHAMBRA·
HALL·OF·THE·AMBASSADORS·

BLACK·ON·
WHITE·

FULL·
SIZE·

GLASS·MLAY·

N.D.N·1809·

PLATE LXXI.

GRANADA.—THE ALHAMBRA.

DETAIL OF GLASS INLAY FROM THE HALL OF THE AMBASSADORS.

THIS little pattern which forms the centre, or eye—the point of departure in fact—of an elaborate geometrical mosaic has been most carefully traced and copied from the original, which yet remains in the centre of the dado on the side of the window on the right of the Sultan's throne in the Hall of the Ambassadors. It may thus be said to occupy an especial post of honour and so to challenge, as it were, curiosity and admiration. Both these a close inspection thoroughly justifies, since in all the history of the manufacture of vitrified substances I know nothing more curious and puzzling. The pattern is in bluish-black on a white ground, and both ground and inlay are made apparently in two separate pieces of glass, and in two only. The most minute inspection shows no joint whatever on the surface of either coloured material; at the same time it establishes the fact that the ground has been made with the whole pattern sunk "en creux," and that the inlay has been made in one piece—practically a specimen of glass lace—and fixed into the cavity of the ground with a very fine calcareous cement, made probably of lime and white of egg. To inlay glass in glass involves little difficulty, if ground and inlay are as it were fused together; but to produce a ground apparently in glass, and to inlay it with so fine a pattern, both " au froid," is a perfect marvel in vitreous manufacture.

The only way in which I can imagine that such an effect could be produced is as follows, but in offering any such explanation I desire to do so with all due deference to practical glass-workers. I believe that two metal-moulds were made one with the ornament in relief, and the other with the same ornament sunk in intaglio. From each mould, glass reproductions having been made of about equal substances (so as to contract equally in cooling), and, with the exception of a black film in one case, of the same glass, the two reproductions were stuck together firmly by the calcareous cement. The black glass in " cameo " would then be encased within the white glass in " intaglio," and the pattern would of course be invisible, the two reproductions being firmly stuck together face to face, making apparently one white glass tessera of double the requisite thickness. The back of the cameo side would then have to be ground away, probably at a lapidary's wheel, until the back of the black pattern in cameo should be reached. At the same moment the face of the white intaglio would be exposed, and the tessera, being reduced to its proper thickness for insertion with the rest of the adjoining glass mosaic, would be fit to permanently combine with it; showing an elaborate black pattern held in by calcareous cement, on a white face, exactly as it now appears.

Any such resolution of a difficult technical problem exhibits the Moors to us as excelling in two of their favourite Arts, viz., inlaying and glass manufacture.

For much of their knowledge of both of these arts there is no doubt that the Moors were indebted to the Arabians. The Arabians were in their turn inheritors from the Byzantine Greeks of many of the traditions of manufacturing excellence once practised by the Romans. Amongst these were, no doubt, almost every process of glass-working and mosaic.* Considerable doubts exist as to either the inheritance by the Greek of the lower empire of the process of inlaying from the Romans, or their originality in adapting the process to their architecture. The first building in which it appears to have been freely used by the Greeks was the Mosque of Santa Sofia, built by Justinian. For that building he is known to have invoked the assistance of Persian designers and artificers, and from the divergence in the patterns of those inlays from any patterns usual in Roman cotemporary work, I am inclined to believe that they represent the foreign element to which I have alluded. A most interesting comparison may be made by the student of the patterns from the Aya Sofia given in Salzenburg's great work, with those of the principal of the Cairene Mosques drawn by Mr. James Wild and given in the "Grammar of Ornament."

---

* For full information on the Glass of the Romans, the Byzantine-Greeks, and the Arabs, of Damascus especially, see Mr. Augustus Franks' account in Mr. J. B. Waring's beautiful work on the Manchester Exhibition, Mr. Alexander Nesbitt's "Historical Notice" Introductory to the Catalogue of Mr. Felix Slade's collection, M. Bontemps' "Guide du Verrier," and M. Labarte's "Histoire des Arts Industriels au moyen-âge et à l'Epoque de la Renaissance."

GRANADA · THE · ALHAMBRA · HALL · OF · THE · AMBASSADORS · MOSAIC · FULL · SIZE ·

PLATE LXXII.

GRANADA.—THE ALHAMBRA.

MOSAIC FROM THE HALL OF THE AMBASSADORS.

IN the description of the last sketch I alluded to the sources whence
the Moors derived much of their knowledge of glass-making,
and mosaic-working. In the specimen now given, the full size of the
original, on the opposite page, a considerable advance is shown upon
what was usual in the contemporary, "Opus Grecanicum," as
executed, either in Italy or in Greece itself. The advance is principally
shown in this particular, that whereas in the last mentioned work, every
complicated pattern is made up out of tesseræ, or glass strips cut into
squares, oblongs, triangles, or other simple figures; in the Moorish
work, arbitrary shapes of considerable geometrical complexity are given
to each separate piece of mosaic. When these tesseræ, so shaped, are
brought together, their combination immediately results in the formation
of perfect patterns, such as the one now illustrated. Tesseræ of this
description were no doubt formed by squeezing plastic clay into metal
moulds, and almost perfect identity was obtained between the tesseræ
obtained from the same mould. These were then apparently covered
with coloured vitreous glazes by a subsequent operation.

In illustration of the advantages possessed by the Moors over the

Greeks, in working such mosaics as the one I have sketched, it may be noted that while a Greek would have required, to make up what is shown, one hundred and nineteen separate pieces, the Moor wanted only forty-nine. Moreover, instead of having to chip every one of the one hundred and nineteen pieces to a definite size and shape, and then to place them slowly so as to ensure the truth of his angles of forty-five and twenty-two and a half degrees, as the Greek or Italian had, the Moor had only to place one of his forty-nine pieces with precision, and, provided he never took any of the eleven patterns, of which his repeats are composed, out of their right turn, his mosaic would work itself with scarcely any other attention on his part. Another source of anxiety was saved to him; viz., constant heedfulness as to the working of the interlacement of his lines—*i. e.* their running, as it were, under and over one another. The result, in this particular, is far clearer and more effective in the Moorish, than according to the Greco-Italian method; since, while in the former there are no joints which do not help to define an interlacement, according to the latter, the joints occurring on the line of mitre of every angle become confused with the joints which express interlacement. A comparison of the Sicilian, with the Alhambrese, geometrical mosaics, would show the superiority of the last mentioned method in a moment.

No people, except perhaps the Chinese, have ever equalled the Moors in devising patterns of most complicated appearance, in which colours were, as it were, counterchanged by combining tiles, or tesseræ, of similar geometrical forms, but made in different tints or tone.

Beautiful examples are given in profusion in the works of Mr. Owen Jones, M. Girault de Prangey, Herr Hessemer, M. Coste and others.

THE·ALHAMBRA· ·LA·SALA·DE·LAS·DOS·HERMANAS·

PLATE LXXIII.

GRANADA—THE ALHAMBRA.

NICHE IN LA SALA DE LAS DOS HERMANAS.

HAT the Moors themselves were fully conscious that in creating the Alhambra they were creating types of beauty for all generations would be clearly manifest from the inscriptions of the Hall of the two Sisters, (from which our illustration is taken), even if every other of the hundreds of inscriptions the building contains in other apartments were destroyed.

"I am the garden, and every morning do I appear decked out in beauty. Look attentively at my elegance, and thou wilt reap the benefit of a commentary on decoration."

"Indeed, we never saw a palace more lofty than this in its exterior, or more brilliantly decorated in its interior; or having more extensive apartments—markets they are, where those provided with money are paid in beauty, and where the judge of elegance is perpetually sitting to pronounce sentence."

"Here is the wonderful cupola, at sight of whose beautiful proportions, all other cupolas vanish and disappear."

Such inscriptions are not all of them of this hyperbolic stamp, since some of them serve to record the names of illustrious founders, and to explain the uses of various parts of the structure. To an inscription of the kind we are indebted for an accurate knowledge of the uses of such niches as the one represented in my sketch. Many travellers and writers had supposed that their purpose had been to hold the slippers of the visitors, but this theory was entirely dispelled when M. Pasqual de Gayangos read the inscription of the left niche of the Hall de las dos Hermanas.

"Praise to God! With my ornaments and tiara* I surpass beauty itself, nay the luminaries in the Zodiac out of envy descend to me.

"The water vase within me, they say, is like a devout man standing towards the Kiblah of the Mihrab,† ready to begin his prayers."

The idea that these niches were used for water-bottles is further strengthened as Mr. Owen Jones has justly remarked, by the existence of the mosaic linings amid the plaster work by which they were surrounded, as well as by the white marble slabs which serve for their base or floor. The wall and pier dados, which extend from these marble slabs to the beautiful Azulejos floor, are all made in elegant mosaic. Above the niche in the sketch appears the ingenious pendentive impost from which spring the great arches carried by the piers, with the characteristic ingrailed fringe work which was almost always retained even, as we see at Seville, in the latest Renaissance Mudejar work.

* Of course alluding to the ceiling, which is even more beautiful in the same style, than that of the Hall of the Abencerrages, which Mr. Owen Jones so perfectly reproduced at Sydenham.

† "The Kiblah is the point in the horizon towards which Mahomedans turn in their prayers marking the place where Mecca stands. The Mihrab is the enclosure before the Kiblah."

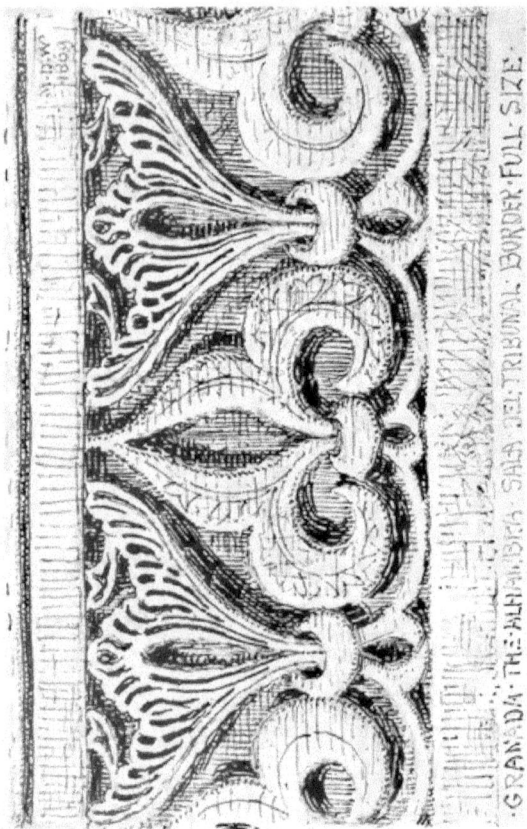

GRANADA · THE·ALHAMBRA · SALA · DE·TRIBUNAL· BORDER· FULL· SIZE·

Plate 74
Granada. — The Alhambra

STUCCO DETAIL FROM THE SALA DEL TRIBUNAL.

THE correctness of this sketch, as to dimension at least, has been ensured by the mode in which it was obtained, viz., by gently pressing a piece of paper against the surface of the piece of ornament (so as to obtain a slight impression of its outline,) then marking it faintly with pencil, pressing it out again quite flat, and finishing it in ink on the spot. It may be looked upon, therefore, as giving, as nearly as is possible on a plane surface, an accurate transcript of the elegant ornament from the Sala del Tribunal selected for illustration. My reason for this selection was, chiefly because I desired to show the minute scale and extreme delicacy of much of the decoration in relief with which the walls of the principal apartments of the Alhambra are covered. It was partly also because this particular specimen retained faint tracing lines drawn, most likely with a silver or lead point, and a free hand, upon the flat surfaces of certain parts of the ornament in relief. These served as guide lines for the yet more delicate labour of the painter, who carried the subdivision of parts, by means of the application of contrasting colours and gilding, into yet more microscopic superficial enrichment.

As this is the last illustration I have to offer of the Alhambra, it may be well to direct the reader's attention briefly to the general system upon which such Art as the Moors practised, and most dearly loved, was based. Those who would know "all about it," must give themselves diligently to a study of all Owen Jones' works; from the ponderous "Alhambra," with its magnificent illustrations, to the little guide to the "Alhambra Courts of the Crystal Palace," not forgetting to test his theory by his practice in the beautiful reproductions of Moorish Art he has created for their edification at Sydenham. In the pages of the smaller volume they will find the system epitomised simply and delightfully in nine propositions under the following heads.

First, to decorate construction, never to construct decoration.

Second, to let all lines grow out of each other in gradual undulations—always so as to conduce to repose.

Third, to care first for general forms and then for harmonious subdivisions and fillings.

Fourth, to balance straight, inclined, and curved forms so as to produce harmony and repose by contrast.

Fifth, to let all lines flow out of a parent stem, traceable throughout its course,

Sixth, either radially (as in nature with the human hand or in a chestnut leaf.)

Seventh, or tangentially,—as stems from branches.

Eighth, to avoid the the simpler curves and use only those of a higher order.

Ninth, to treat all ornament conventionally, i.e., not in direct imitation of Nature, but in a mode of imitation subordinated to the architectural conditions of the surface or form to be ornamented.

GRANADA

CATHEDRAL FROM THE BACK OF THE HIGH ALTAR.

Plate 75

Granada.

VIEW OF THE CATHEDRAL FROM THE BACK OF THE HIGH ALTAR

IT is always interesting to watch the first rays of light which dissipate clouds of darkness or prejudice; and this, by the aid of the annals of the early printing press, we are enabled to do (with comparative certainty as to chronology) in the case of the dawn of the revival of classical architecture in every country of Europe except Italy. In that favoured land, the sacred fire of Roman tradition was never quite extinguished, and in its great cities the renascent flame was already lambent, and gaining strength, before Sweynheim and Pannarz started their celebrated press at Subiaco.

The first edition of the ten books of Vitruvius printed by G. Herolt at Rome, *circa* 1486, was immediately followed by the edition of Florence, under the editorship of Leon Baptista Alberti, bearing the imprint of the previous year. At least two other editions were exhausted in Italy before the close of the century, and succeeded by many more previous to the middle of the sixteenth century.

Alberti's own admirable writings on Architecture and the other Fine Arts moved all Italy, giving a thoroughly practical direction to the lessons somewhat obscurely inculated by Vitruvius; whose writings, without Alberti's comments, would have been of little practical use in countries in which ample remains of classical art were not at hand for reference and study.

The first French edition of the text of Vitruvius is of 1523; the first German is of 1543. The first French translation dates from 1547; the first German from 1548, published at Nuremburg. It was "volgarizzato" in Italy from 1521.

The Latin text was translated into Spanish by Miguel de Urrea and printed after his death at Alcala de Heñares in 1587. Its publication had however been long preceded in Spain by the digest of the views of Vitruvius under the title of "las Medidas del Romano o Vitruvio," published by Diego de Sagredo in 1526. Sagredo had no doubt been stimulated to such studies, (as Alberti had previously been) by his admiration of the vestiges of Roman architectural greatness, still abounding on the soil of his native land.

What oral tradition could teach previous to the publication of these texts in Spain, no doubt the architect of the Cathedral of Granada, Diego de Siloe, had learnt from his father, Gil, the even more celebrated Sculptor of Burgos; whose monuments to Don Juan II., his Queen, Donna Isabel, and the Infante Don Alonso, and whose "Retablo" in the Cartuja of Miraflores in the outskirts of that city, have never been surpassed in tasteful elaboration.* From whatever source Diego de Siloe may have obtained his knowledge, certain it is that he must share with Alonso Covarrubbias, the honour of having been the earliest revivers of classical architecture in Spain: not in its details only as had been attempted by the early

* See Mr. J. B. Waring's masterly sketches of the detail of these works of art.

Plateresque architects, but in its structural proportions and in its symmetrical arrangements of great leading features. The following is the account of the construction of this Cathedral given by Amirola.*

"It was begun," he says, "on the 15th of March, 1529, and consists of three naves, the principal of which terminates in the choir after the Gothic manner. It is four hundred and twenty-five feet (Spanish) long, and two hundred and forty-nine wide. The order is Corinthian, but defective in its true proportions, since the principal nave is only forty-five feet wide, its height is one hundred and twenty." It would profit us but little to follow Amirola through his straight-laced criticisms on a design the beauty of which he was unable to apprehend ; and it may be well to take a larger and juster view of its merits. The following which, I heartily endorse, is the verdict of a far better judge.† " Looking at its plan only, this is certainly one of the finest churches in Europe. It would be difficult to point out any other in which the central aisle leads up to the dome, so well proportioned to its dimensions, and to the dignity of the high altar which stands under it, or one where the side aisles have a purpose and a meaning so perfectly appropriate to the situation, and where the centre aisle has also its functions as perfectly marked out and so well understood. All this being so, it is puzzling to know how it has been so neglected."

My sketch has been taken from the "Ambulatory" at the back

* Who also states that in his time the drawings of the design by Diego Siloe were yet extant, " Noticias de los Arquitectos y Arquitectura de España." Madrid. 1829. Vol. I. page 199.

† " History of the Modern Styles of Architecture," by James Fergusson. London. 1862. page 135.

of, and surrounding, the choir. Its dimensions, as will be at once apparent, are enormous. The arches, which separate the choir from the ambulatory, and through one of which in my sketch the high altar is seen, are of very great interest. They form the earliest examples I have ever seen (out of Italy) of artificial perspectives, "guocchi di prospettiva." The arches next to the choir are narrower and lower than those next to the ambulatory; the distance between the two, owing to the necessities of supporting and distributing the weights of the vast cupola, being very considerable. The two archways are connected by falling lines of impost mouldings and converging lines of coffering. The consequence is that, as appears in the sketch, the archways, which really occupy only about five and twenty feet in depth, look at least double that dimension.

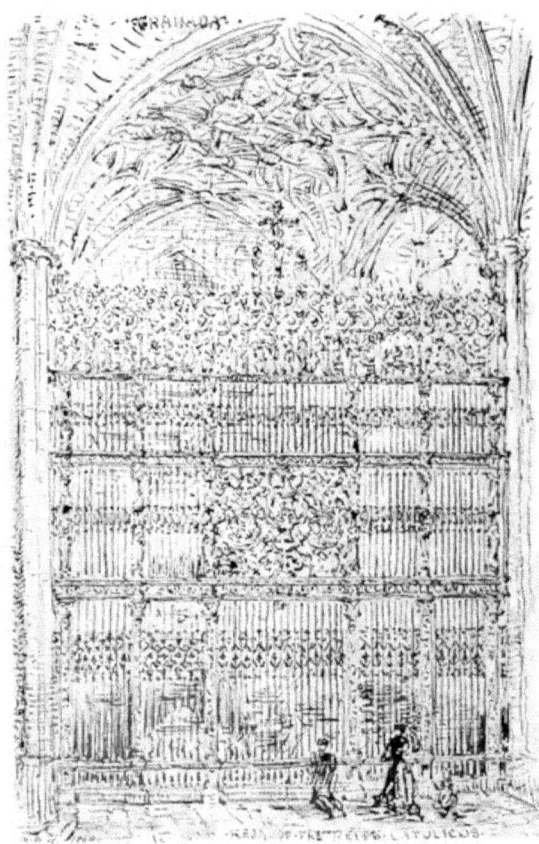

GRANADA

REJA DE LOS REYES CATÓLICOS

Plate 76

Granada

THE REJA OF THE REYES CATOLICOS.

I WAS tempted to sketch this magnificent screen for four reasons :—

Firstly, because it is, I believe, entirely of iron, which most of the Spanish Rejas are not.

Secondly, because it is, I also believe, the earliest specimen of anything like equal importance in Spain.

Thirdly, because of its historical interest in enclosing the tombs of " the Catholic Sovereigns " on the spot before which the greatness of their lives had been achieved.

Fourthly, because I considered it to be the best in design of all I saw.

It is by no means the richest, but it appeared to me to be arranged upon the justest principles. Its chief merits, as compared with many others, I considered to be as follows :—

Firstly, its *transparency*. One of the most important qualities any such screen should possess, is that of due subordination to the great architectural features of the locality in which it it is placed. Where ornament is spread all over the surface of a screen, or where the main lines wander about in capricious directions, the eye is arrested by the metal work as a plane surface ; and if not actually stopped by it, is at least led off in wayward directions, and fails to pass beyond it.   In this case, the rectangularity of the whole gives great repose ; the plain vertical bars almost disappear ; while the splendidly ornamented portions of the screen seem as if suspended in mid air, and in no wise injure the effect of the architecture,* or diminish the apparent space of the locality they decorate.

Secondly, its *stability* without heaviness.   The subdivision of the whole surface into regular compartments allows of a concentration of strength in the skeleton lines, and gives great constructional stiffness without too much formality.

Thirdly, its *propriety of design*.   Its author has simply, as it were, asserted the principle of " serve God and honour the King ;" instead of, as is usual, " look at me, and see what a fine fellow I am."   At the summit of his design he has represented the Crucifixion ; immediately beneath, the leading incidents of Gospel history, making conspicuous (in compliment no doubt to the triumph of the Church in the entry into Granada of his sovereigns), Christ's entry into Jerusalem.   As the central object, not much less than twenty feet square, he has grouped in masterly style the full heraldic insignia of those whose remains are deposited in the chapel beyond.   The lower portion of his design has evidently been intended simply to give stability to the upper part, and to

* Mr. Street in referring to the usual practice in good mediæval iron screens observes that in such " the ornament is reserved for open traceried crestings, with bent and sharply cut crockets, for traceried rails, and for the locks and fastenings."   He mentions a very fine iron screen, thirty feet high, as existing at Pamplona, the general design of which seems to have a good deal in common with that of the " Reja de los Reyes" at Granada.   It appears, however, to be of earlier date, and consequently more decidedly Gothic in character.

close the access to the magnificent marble and alabaster monuments of Ferdinand and Isabella, and of Philip of Burgundy and " Juana la Loca," without interfering with the facilities for seeing them of those who might gain access to the Antechapel, but be refused it to the Mausoleum itself.

The name of the admirable artist, " el Maestre Bartholomé," who wrought this Reja in the year 1522, is inscribed upon it, near to the keyhole of the great central gates.

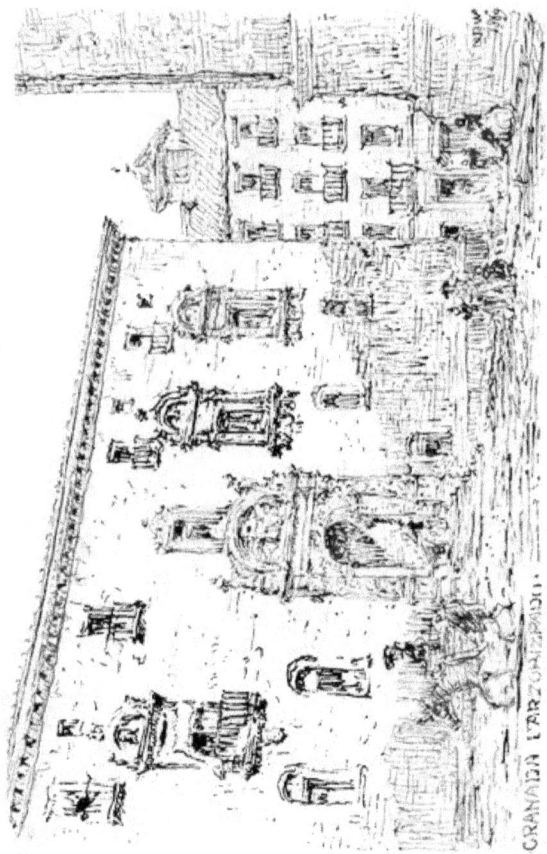

GRANADA PIAZZIPPADI

Plate 77

Granada.

VIEW OF THE ARZOBISPADO.

A CAREFUL contrast of this stately old mansion in which, if not the hand, at least the influence of the architect, Henrique de Egas, (son of Anequin de Egas de Bruselas, so greatly patronized by the celebrated Cardinal Mendoza,) may be clearly traced, with the great Palace of Charles V., ascribed to the artist Machuca, (both at Granada,) may afford a useful lesson to the architectural student. In the earliest of the two monuments—the Arzobispado—a window of which I now offer a slight sketch, the florid Plateresque style, as exemplified by the celebrated Hospedal de la Santa Cruz, at Toledo, (Sketches 44, 45, 46) is at once recalled to the memory. In the latest, we find a marked sympathy with the symmetrical style of the then fashionable Italian architects. The Circular Cortile of Vignola's masterpiece at Caprarola, is exceeded in dimension, and indeed in dignity of style, by the vast round Patio of the Palace of Charles V., with which it is probably nearly contemporary.

Such sober architecture, though enriched by the chisel of sculptors who, like Berruguete, had been ardent admirers of Florentine and Roman models, was the form of Plateresque which, intervening between the first form of Renaissance, founded on French and Burgundian models, and the austere Italian of Herrera, found special favour in the eyes of the most judicious critics in Spain.

How far the best designers of Spain, amongst whom must certainly be reckoned Juan de Arfe y Villafañe, acknowledged their dependence upon the great Italian masters for all they considered most excellent in style, may be gathered from the curious account of the development of good art in his time* that he gives in his celebrated Treatise on Sculpture and Architecture. After dwelling upon what he curiously enough calls the " obra moderna," with which the great cathedrals of Spain had been, as he considers, built, he observes, " This *barbarous work*, having arrived at its end, its disuse having commenced in our times, gave place to the ancient styles of the Greeks and Romans. Although this style of work had been revived at an earlier period in Italy by the diligence and study of Bramante, Master of the Works of St. Peter's at Rome, Baldassare Perruzzi and Leon Baptista Alberti, celebrated architects, it also began to flourish in Spain through the industry of the excellent Alonso de Covarrubbias, Master of the Works of the Cathedral at Toledo, and of the Royal Palace, father of the most famous doctor, Don Diego Covarrubbias, President of the Supreme Council of his Majesty and Bishop of Segovia, and of Diego Siloe, Master of the Works of the Cathedral and Palace of Granada. These masters began to use this kind of work in many places wherever they built, although always with some admixture of the *modern* work (Gothic or early Plateresque) which they could never entirely forget."

* " Varia Commensuracion." Sixth Edition, pages 111—122.

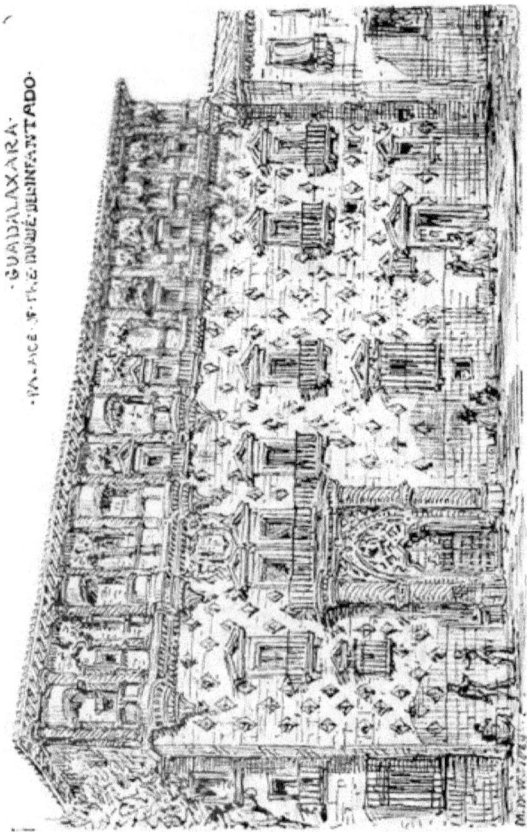

·GUADALAXARA·
·PALACE OF THE DUKE DELINFANTADO·

Plate 78.

Guadalaxara.

PALACIO DE LOS DUQUES DEL INFANTADO.

THIS is unquestionably one of the most important of the Palaces of the ancient nobility left in Spain, worthy of the renown of the Mendozas, long Seigneurs of Guadalaxara. In spite of its present picturesque aspect, however, architecturally speaking, it is a strange jumble of incongruities; and offers but a ghost of the beauty it must have possessed upon its first construction towards the end of the fifteenth century from 1461 onwards. Splendour it must have possessed in perfection at the date at which it excited warm admiration in the breast of the captive sovereign, Francis I. of France, who was here magnificently entertained by the then Duque del Infantado. The top story with its remains of continuous arcading and balconies, the walls, the splendid doorway, and above all the Patio, with the exception probably of the top cornice and the Doric columns of the ground-floor arcade, all belong to the original construction. These remains afford sufficient indication of what has been destroyed to make way for Italian decoration and barbarous repair, to enable the practised eye to see the whole as it once existed; before a vulgar desire for novelty, and especially for foreign novelty induced the desecration of the integrity of the design. One might have fancied that every true Spaniard would have regarded this palace almost as a holy place, from its having received the last breath of the great Cardinal Mendoza—the " Rex tertius," whom Felipe Vigarny, or some other dextrous sculptor, portrayed in the carvings of the Cathedral at Granada,* riding with Ferdinand and Isabella, and receiving the keys of the Alhambra from the hands of the unfortunate " Boabdil el Chico."

The interior of this Palace is fully as rich and remarkable as the exterior. The Patio which is about eighty feet long by fifty-six wide, (about two-thirds of the size of the court-yards of the Royal Exchange and the India Office), is surrounded by arcades of two stories, each about twenty feet in height. Both series of arches are of a Gothic and fantastic form, with spandrels filled in on the lower story with lions, and on the upper with winged griffins. Between each arch are columns, surmounted with armorial bearings, eagles, and grouped finials. The whole, if coarsely, is very spiritedly carved, and produces a stately and simple, though rich effect. The saloons are large and lofty, with remains of beautiful half Moorish ceilings, and much effective Italian fresco decoration of good colour and enriched with harmonious Arabesque ornament.

The state of this once splendid structure is unfortunately as dilapidated as the national finances. What more can or need be said ? Everything going to pieces for want of that " stitch in time," which nowhere, and in nothing, in Spain, seems ever likely " to save nine."

* Casts of these sculptures I caused to be placed in the surface of the Renaissance Court of the Crystal Palace.

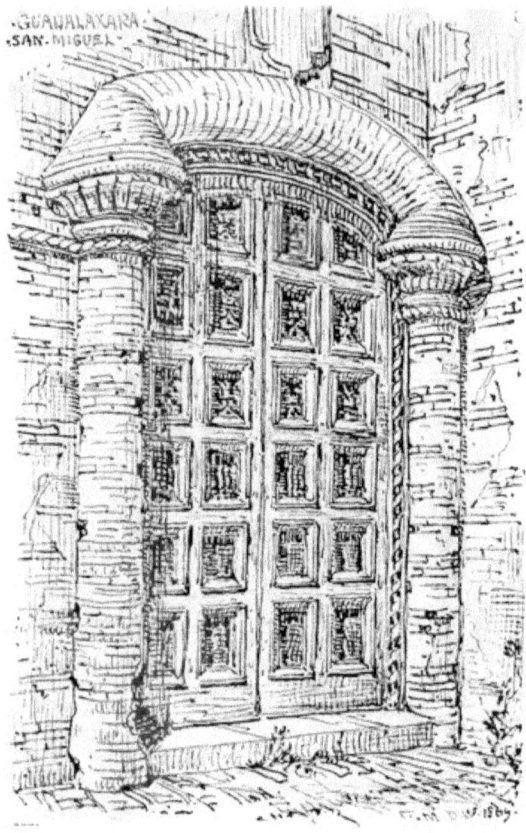

GUADALAXARA
SAN MIGUEL

Plate 79.

Guadalaxara.

DOORWAY OF THE MONASTERY OF SAN MIGUEL.

IN and about Guadalaxara may be found many indications of the traditional preservation, long after the expulsion of the Moors, not only from New Castille, but from Spain generally as well, of their excellence in the technical arts, amongst which brick-making, combining, and laying were conspicuous. Hence, especially throughout the two Castilles, Aragon, and Andalucia, the common method of using brick-work is peculiarly Oriental and effective. The entrance doorway to the Monastery of San Miguel, which forms the subject of our seventy-ninth sketch, illustrates this mixture; as well it may, since traces are yet to be found of the structure having been originally a mosque converted, probably, shortly before the year 1500 to Christian uses. The round instead of square buttresses, with conical terminations, the segmental arch, with its ponderous archivolt, the great strength and almost heaviness given by the regular rectangular setting out of the woodwork—and a coarseness and yet spirit in the execution of carving, are marked features of Aragonese style; the echoes of which may not unfrequently be met with at Naples, especially in the entrance gateways to many an old house. I well remember being puzzled by several of those which I sketched there, and which appeared to me to differ from ordinary contemporary Italian architecture in other localities. I subsequently recognized similar features in Palermo, and elsewhere in Sicily.

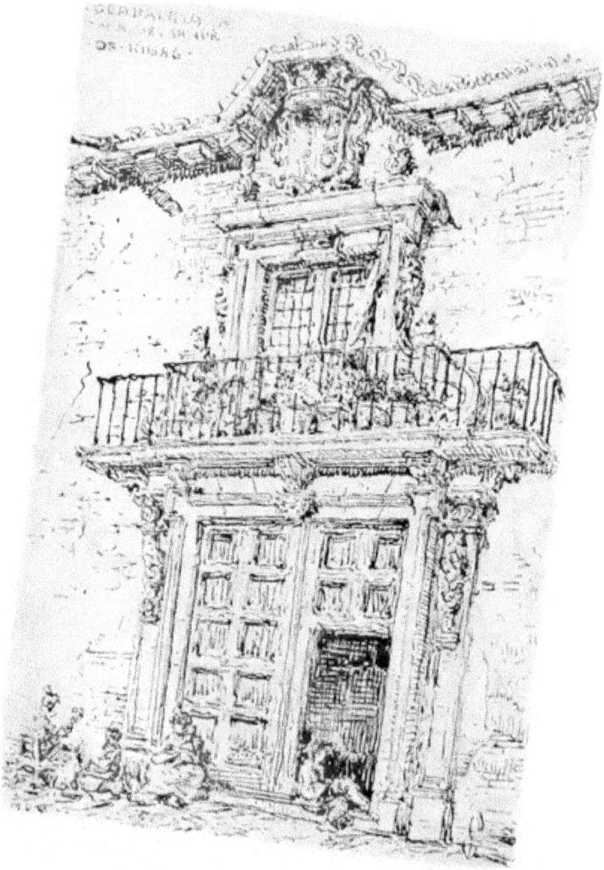

PLATE LXXX.

GUADALAXARA.

CASA DEL DUQUÉ DE RIBAS.

THE traveller who takes his seat for an hour or so before some old portal of a Spanish provincial mansion, garnished with heraldic insignia, proclaiming the rank, if not the dignity, of the possible owner, can scarcely fail to be struck by the usual incongruity between the assumption of the structure, and the modesty, not to say meanness, of those who pass in and out of it generally at long intervals. The sketcher's operations naturally, after a little while, attract the attention of some few, and "their name is legion" throughout Spain, of those who have nothing to do; or who, at any rate, do nothing, but wander lazily but restlessly up and down to while away the time. After a compliment or two, and probably a request that the spectators will not stand exactly between the artist and the object he may be drawing, an inquiry very generally follows as to "whose house that may be?" If the answer extends beyond the usual "Quien sabe Caballero?" it may chance to be "del Señor Duqué," or "del Señor Marques," something or other, or at any rate of a "Señor somebody," "somebody," "somebody." To the next inquiry, as to where the Hidalgo, if he be such, may be? the usual answer will be "Madrid" or "Paris," or at any rate the "chef-

lieu" of the Province. The next demand may likely enough be, "Who
lives there then, now?" If the answer is not the usual "No puedo decir
a Usted," it may possibly be, "El Señor Administrador," the Steward, or
"Algunos Pobres," or "Don Manoel, the shoemaker," or "Don Juan, the
carpenter."

Where the nobility live, if they are not all absentees, it seems
very difficult to find out; and hence it is that instead of ladies
and gentlemen, and liveried servants, who pass in and out of these
grand looking "portone," the sketcher usually sees only extremely
picturesque poverty. Sometimes this presents itself in the shape of a
ragged girl or two, carrying antique-shaped earthen water-jars, sometimes an old woman with a heap of long-haired unkempt children
sitting down to spin, or reel off yarn, or lolling against the wall, distaff
in hand; and sometimes, possibly, two or three boys or young men
assemble, who, after smoking out some cigarrilos or stumps of cigars,
coil themselves up on the threshold, and go off into a comatose
condition closely resembling sleep.

Such were my experiences whilst trying to gain some local information as to the mansion of the very noble, the Duqué de Ribas at
Guadalaxara.

GUADALAXARA. DOOR-HANDLE.

CALLE·DEL·BARRIO·NUEVO·Nº15·

PLATE LXXXI.

GUADALAXARA.

DOOR HANDLE FROM THE CALLE DEL BARRIO NUEVO.

THE outskirts of Guadalaxara are very picturesque, and the traveller who wanders about in quest of beauty, old or new, cannot fail to be rewarded; not only by glimpses of scenery, but by the discovery of many quaint little fragments of art which have escaped the attention of the many despoiling locusts—native as well as foreign—who have done their best at different times to "devour the land." Of such, a specimen is given in the " knowing " little knocker, or door-handle illustrated in my eighty-first sketch. It is no doubt a joke on the part of some cunning smith, of the last century, mindful of the still greater cunning of his handicraft, traditions of which may have descended to him, from the days when the armourers of Spain rivalled those of Milan and Augsburg.

PLATE LXXXII.

SARAGOSSA.

VIEW OF THE PATIO OF THE PALACIO DE LA INFANTA.

PONZ speaks with great complacency of the sumptuousness of the houses of Saragossa—particularly those with columns, (such as that of the Marques de Monistol) and those the Patios of which are adorned with sculptures—" such costly and sumptuous works," he says, " as no one undertakes now a days." Amongst these he particularises the house which forms the subject of the present sketch. Before his time it appears to have belonged to the Citizen Gabriel Zaporta, " muy distinguido y rico," as Ponz calls him. From him it was bought by the widow of a certain Don Gabriel Franco. At the close of the last century it was the home of the Infante Don Luis, (uncle of Charles IV. of Spain), a Cardinal and Archbishop of Toledo! who married " La Vallabriga," earning exile to Saragossa for his pains. She lived here with him, and procured for the house its popular and best known name, la Casa de la Infanta. Their eldest daughter was bestowed, as an Infanta of Spain, upon the detestable Godoy—" Prince of Peace,"—the recognised lover of her first cousin by marriage, the Queen, wife of Charles IV., thus crowning a double mésalliance.

"On the ground floor," says Ponz,[*] "of the Patio are twelve

* Viage de España. Vol. XV. page 79.

arches supported on columns wrought with a thousand fancies, as are those also of the first floor. On the lower floor of this house is a painter's studio. Both floors are enriched with medallions representing kings, fanciful foliage, and infinite labour in cornices, mouldings, &c." Similar elaboration, now much defaced, is to be seen in the staircase with vaulting, and handrail with medallions recalling those of the first floor.

Amongst the most important palaces, next to the house of Zaporta or de la Infanta, and that of the Marques de Monistol, were those known as the "Castel-Florit," which belonged in Ponz's time to the Count Aranda—and another the property of the Duqué de Hijar. The "Casa de Comercio" which forms the subject of my eighty-fifth sketch was less important as to quantity, but more important as to quality, than those last mentioned appear to have been. As a general rule, the Saragossan houses appear very large but coarsely treated as to detail, even in the richest, such as those with showy windows behind the Seminario, in the Plazuela de San Carlos.

My sketch sufficiently shows the "base uses" to which the truly palatial Casa de Zaporta, or de la Infanta, has "come at last." It is well that as many as possible of the rising generation of art-students should see it, for it is not likely that any of it will be left for their children.

CASA
DE
LOS INFANTES
ZARAGOZA

PLATE LXXXIII.

SARAGOSSA.

DETAIL OF THE ARCADING OF THE FIRST FLOOR OF THE CASA DE LA INFANTA.

THIS sketch gives to an enlarged scale some of the architectural features represented in little in the preceding sketch. Many of the arches which were once open in a beautiful arcading are now closed up in lath and plaster; with a heartless indifference to everything else than getting as much room as possible to let to the poor lodgers who swarm in this once splendid Palace. The whitewash brush goes recklessly over any surfaces with which it is brought into contact at the command of sanitary inspectors, who enforce perfunctory cleansings from time to time of at least the "outside of the platter." As I sat sketching and "poking about" for some hours in this apparent "rabbit warren" of a house, I could not but become conscious that the Arragonese had by no means lost their old character for devotion, not to say bigotry. "Our Lady of the pillar," the tutelary of Saragossa in spite of all alleged pilferings from her shrine, seemed still at a premium in popular estimation; and casts of her in the poorest plaster were multiplied even in the poorest tenements. In fact, this seemed to be the very place for meeting with the truly Spanish couple of the lower middle class, so well sketched by the German Fischer in his travels at the close of the last

century. "I cannot conclude this letter," says he, "without saying a
word or two of my hosts. Both the man and his wife are originals not
to be met with but in Catholic countries ; both bigots to excess, but
each in a different way. In the husband, this disposition has assumed
a silent and gloomy cast of character, while in his wife it bears all
the symptoms of tenderness. The husband has filled the whole house,
and especially his own apartment, with images of saints, resembling
an entire collection of the little Augsburg toys so well known in Germany.
In fulfilment of a vow, he mutters his prayers three times a day before
these idols, an occupation which daily employs two full hours. He also
imposes on himself very painful mortifications, talks very little, reads
gloomy books, and remains whole hours with his eyes shut, so that
he is on the high road to become either a madman or a saint. The
wife's fanaticism is much more social, and her pious imaginations
bear the stamp of the mildness and softness of her sex. She has got
herself received a "slave of the Holy Trinity" (esclava de la
Santissima Trinidad), of which she has obtained a certificate in form
from her confessor, and in consequence of which she is bound every
day to decorate a large picture with flowers and tapers, to repeat a
certain number of prayers before it, and to pay a certain sum weekly to
her confessor, an agent of the Trinity; yet all this does not seem
to her sufficient for salvation, and she has besides an image of the Holy
Virgin, which she very punctually supplies with all the necessary
habiliments, both for day and night, besides tapers, flowers and all that
can contribute to ornament the happy idol.

"This devout esclava is a little woman very affable and complaisant,
whose religious sentiments do not at all interfere with other terrestrial
feelings, while her impassive husband seems to have arrived at all
the spirituality of the blessed."

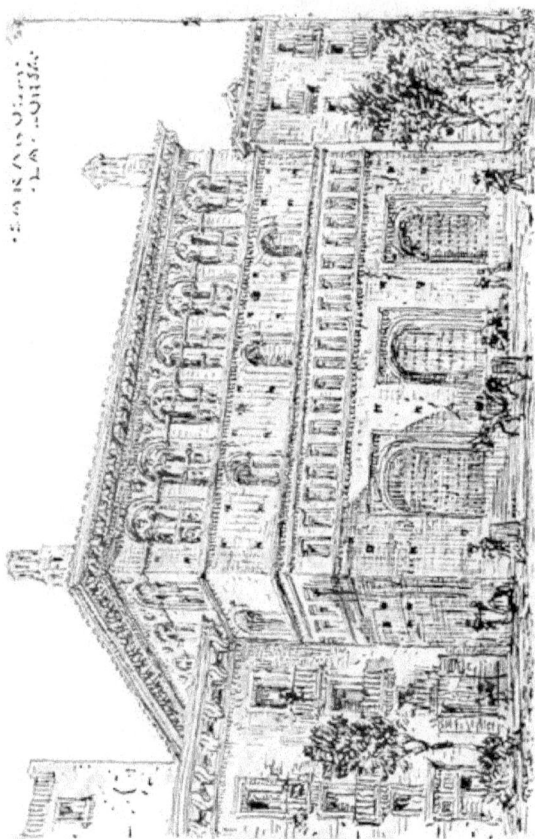

PLATE LXXXIV.

SARAGOSSA.

EXTERIOR OF THE EXCHANGE.

THERE is something about the exterior of this fine building essentially Florentine in style. The bold overhanging and crowning cornice, the Ricardi-Palace kind of windows, the simplicity of the Mezzanine, and indeed the introduction of a Mezzanine at all, associated with the severity of the rectangular structure, massive in a noble simplicity, rather recall the work of the grand masters of Tuscan Architecture at the end of the fifteenth century, than any styles, Plateresque or Greco-Roman, one recognises as peculiarly Spanish.

The name of the architect appears to have been lost, but there is no question as to the date of its erection, which is given by an inscription which runs beneath a cornice in the interior, and states that it was completed in "1551, reynando Donña Joana y Don Carlos su hijo."

The "Lonjas," or Exchanges, of Spain, constitute an important and interesting class of buildings, dating, from mediæval times in the most commercial of the towns on the seaboard, and from the Renaissance period in those of the interior. The term Lonja, originally only implied a "long place" or platform, the sort of spot in a town

on which merchants would meet, as on "the flags" at Liverpool. In
process of time the Lonjas came to be covered in, and converted into
handsome "Exchanges." The earliest structure of this class is, or
rather was, at Barcelona. All the fine old building of 1383, Mr.
Street tells us, has "been completely destroyed, with the one exception
of its grand Hall, which still does service as of old. This consists of
three naves, divided by lofty and slender columns, which carry stilted
semi-circular arches. The ceiling is flat . . . . and the dimensions
about one hundred feet by seventy five." The "Casa Lonja" of
Valencia, which Mr. Street has also fully illustrated* is one of the
prettiest of the late Gothic buildings in Spain. It was erected between
1482 and the close of the fifteenth century. The next important
Lonja in point of date was the Saragossan of 1551. The last
was that of Seville built by Herrera between 1585 and 1598, and
certainly one of his best works. It was avowedly built in rivalry with
Gresham's Royal Exchange—completed in 1571.

To the interior of the fine building under notice I could not
obtain access, and have therefore to trust to Ponz's description of it.
" It forms," he says, " a splendid saloon with an internal double gallery
of Doric columns and arches, to the number of fifty." Within it
are erected an altar to, and statue of, the guardian angel, in fact the
building had its Lararium. Ponz mentions, further, many paintings.
These appear no longer to exist, since all I could learn by personal
inquiry on the spot was that the place, having long been used as a
carpenter's shop and warehouse was now absolutely empty and unused.
I fear therefore that the "Angelo Custode" has had too much to do,
and has broken down under his task.

* "Gothic Architecture in Spain," page 270.

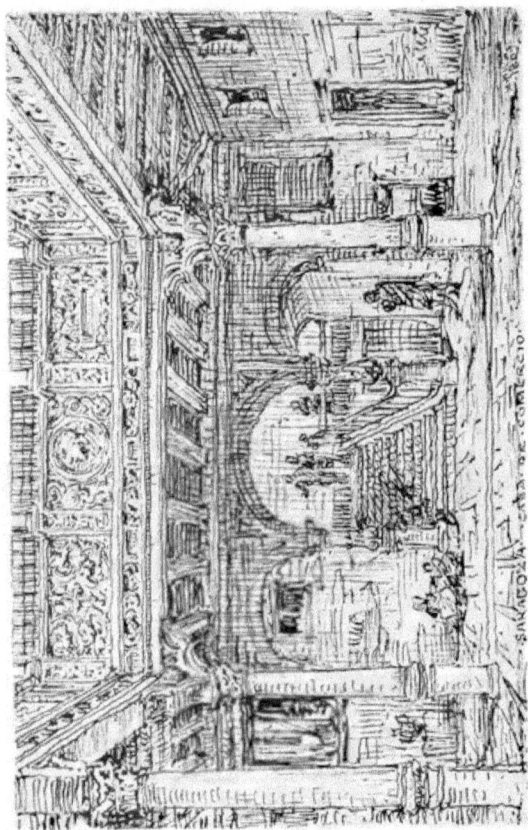

PLATE LXXXV.

SARAGOSSA.

PATIO OF THE CASA DE COMERCIO.

THIS house, originally a Gothic one, in some of its earliest details, still acknowledges its allegiance to the noble family of the Torrellas, its founders. Their arms, with a lion, and the three little towers which pun heraldically upon their name, as charges, still exist upon a Gothic escutcheon over one of the doorways. The house is locally stated, I know not on what authority, to have been occupied, and altered by a company of Genoese merchants, whence, no doubt, its popular name "de Comercio." It is situated in the Calle de Sant, Jago, and is now the property of the Marquis de Ayerve.

Although retaining the usual Saragossan bracket-capitals, and "Anillos" in the shape of quasi bases and dies or pedestals united, the symmetry of the plan, and the regularity of the cinque-cento ornament and Arabesque of the panels and pilasters, certainly bear out the tradition of the Genoese occupation and alteration of an original mediæval structure, early in the sixteenth century.

At that time, and for nearly a couple of centuries afterwards, the bulk of the commercial transactions of Spain were administered by foreigners, principally at first Italians, and subsequently Flemings and Frenchmen.

The expulsion of the Moors, the persecutions of the Jews, and the pouring in of American silver opened up a splendid field in Spain, during this period, for the trafficking talents of people endowed with greater activity and commercial genius, than the Spaniards themselves possessed. Their function was to despise trade, and use, but detest, the foreigners, whose aptitude for work supplied the wants engendered by one of their besetting sins—laziness. " Ociedad, raiz de los vicios, y sepulchro de las virtudes," as Marcos Obregon exclaims. " En quatro cosas," he continues, " gasta la vida el ocioso, en dormir sin tiempo, en comer sin sagon, en solicitar quietas, en murmurar de todos."[*]

The following are the Countess d'Aulnois' comments on the effects of the mixed jealousy and laziness of the Spaniards in her time—the latter part of the seventeenth century.

" All strangers," she says, " what services soever they may have done, the Spaniards ought to fear them, they considering themselves and interests only, in such a manner that the Italians and Flemings, that are this king's subjects, are used no more favourably than if born under another master. If they pretend to imployments, either at Court or in the armies, they are told they are not natural Spaniards who engross all, as well to keep up the glory of the nation, as out of diffidence of others, whom they in a manner declare incapable of all trust because not born in Spain ; this country, nevertheless, abounds in strangers, but they are only artificers and mercenaries invited by gain, and that meddle with nothing but their peddling traffick. It is thought that there are above forty thousand French in Madrid, who, wearing the Spanish habit, and calling themselves Burgundinians, Walloons and Lorraines, keep up commerce and manufacture ; it concerns them to

[*] " Marcos Obregon por el Maestro Vicente Espinel." Madrid. 1804. Pages 40—41.

conceal their country, for if it be discovered, they are obliged to pay a daily Pole-money of about a penny to the town, and, any bad success happening to the publick, appearing in the streets, are liable to a thousand insolencies, even to blows.

"They that know what number of strangers are in this town, report, that would they undertake it, they might make themselves masters, and drive out the Spaniards."

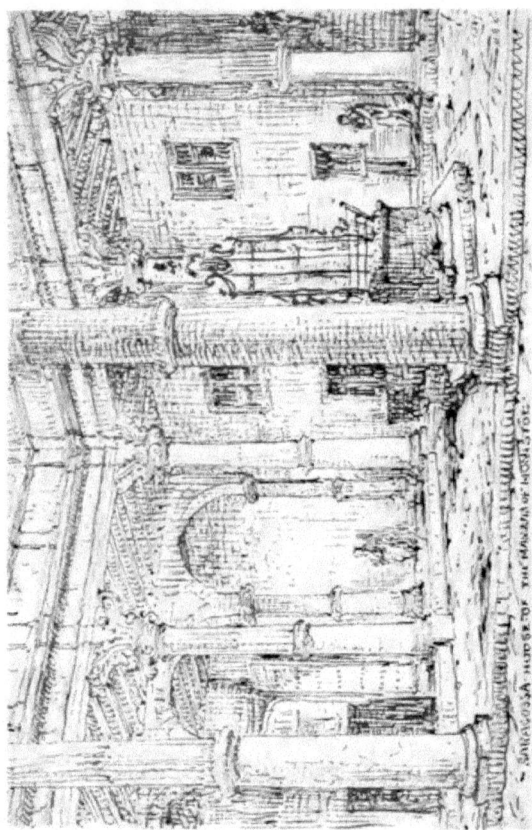

SARAGOSSA. HOUSE OF THE MANZANA MISERICORDIA.

PLATE LXXXVI.

PATIO OF THE HOUSE OF THE MARQUIS OF MONISTOL.

THE great dimensions of this house, and its massive strength and solidity are no bad emblems of the old sturdiness, wealth, and pride of the Aragonese nobility, whose Plateresque architecture "differed" as Mr. O'Shea justly remarks, "in many points from its countertype the Seville Moro-Italian, or strictly Andalusian style, applied to private dwellings." Although apparently far ruder in execution than either of the other two houses I sketched—that of the Infanta and that known as de Comercio—in the same city I have little doubt that this is of considerably later date. The florid Spanish Plateresque of the former, and the cinque-cento carving of the latter, took precedence of the more regular Greco-Roman architecture aimed at by the architect of the house now under notice. The retention of the bracket capital in lieu of either arches or a lengthened column, and of the "anillo" or ring dividing the shaft into two heights, illustrate the way in which local habits interfered with the adoption of the rigid rules prescribed by the writers on architecture, and practised by contemporary architects, of the Herrera type.

Considering the terrible "fortunes of war," to which Saragossa has been exposed, and its frightful hand to hand fighting in the heart of the city, it is only wonderful that so much of the past should still linger within the lines of defence. If the ruinous sieges have left Saragossa poorer than they found her, they certainly do not appear to have left her weaker or less fierce. She struck me as being poorer and prouder than any other city I visited in Spain. At the same time, both men and women show a hardy activity and lively inclination to pugnacity I did not see elsewhere. The only answer I got from a Madrileño to my question as to "why the Saragossans did not work?" was, that "they preferred fighting," adding that "while they would look hard at a peseta before they would undertake even a trifling job for it, they would at any time do a good day's fighting for one half of that coin."

·SARAGOZA·
·PLAZUELA·ADUANA·

P⟋ATE L∧II. ~~XXXⱱ.~~

SARAGOSSA.

BRONZE RENAISSANCE KNOCKER OF A HOUSE IN THE PLAZUELA ADUANA.

THE quant little animal, or rather conventionalised notion of an animal, which I found in an out of the way "Plazuela," or "little place," of Saragossa, doing duty as a knocker, furnishes a good illustration of the ready dexterity in his craft of the old Spanish smith and brazier. Of splendid bronze work (in spite of the intrinsic value of the material which has no doubt led to the fusion of thousands of treasures of Art all over the Peninsula) Spain yet possesses invaluable treasures. Amongst these the most salient which occur to my memory as single pieces, are the magnificent eleven gilt life-size portrait statues of the greatest of the Spanish Royal Family from Charles V. to Philip II. with which Pompeio Leoni decorated the "Entierros Reales" of the Escorial—and the same sculptor's still finer statues of the celebrated prime minister and favourite, the Duqué de Lerma, and his Duqueza, founders of the Convent of San Pablo, at Valladolid, whence they have been transferred to the museum of that city. As great semi-architectural, semi-sculpturesque works in bronze, occasionally with an admixture of iron, of course the most important and abundant are the late Rejas, or metal screens, of the great Spanish churches and cathedrals. Of these ample notices are given by both Ford and O'Shea—authorities, at once so excellent, and so readily accessible, as to render unnecessary any more on my part than a passing reference to them.

Another form in which copper and bronze have have been well and plentifully used by the Spaniards is in the shape of coverings and strengthenings to doors. In this shape the models have been mainly derived from the Moors whose doors may generally, whether in wood or metal, be regarded as perfection itself, for beauty, strength, and fitness for the circumstances under which they have been used. The Spaniards (at Toledo Cathedral for example) have produced many admirable doors in which, by the judicious strengthening of the joiner's work with embossed and occasionally perforated bronze plates, they have combined strength with moderate substance, and the appearance of great richness with fairly simple and not costly labour.

PLATE ⚔ LXXXVIII. /

LÉRIDA.

TOWER OF THE CHURCH OF SAN LORENZO.

THE interest of every other building in Lerida altogether pales before that of its noble, but now much desecrated Cathedral. Its ancient glories may be well studied in Mr. Street's pages, but its present humiliation can only be appreciated upon the spot. Toiling up from the city through streets and open platforms on the hill-side, thronged with soldiers, gipsies, beggars, and ragged boys innumerable, the traveller at last arrives, not at a church, but at a monster-barrack. In lieu of a sacristan he has to engage the services of a corporal as Cicerone, and with the consent of, I am bound to say, an exceedingly polite Spanish officer, he is free to examine, at his leisure, a Cathedral which, as Mr. Street says, " is in itself worth the journey from England." Its construction, and that of its splendid cloister, occupied almost the whole of the thirteenth century, and the vastness and regularity of its plan, its solid and perfect execution, and the just proportion of its structural and ornamental details certainly, to my mind, justify the praise bestowed upon them by that accomplished architect.

It was really sad to see such a building cut about by the insertion of floors and partitions, and to hear the piquant, not to say ribald, jokes, "refranes, seguidillas" and songs of the soldiers, echoing from vaulting which once rang only with peals from the organ, and chants and hymns from the priests and people.

As my stay was bound to be short in Lerida, and I remembered that Mr. Street had done full justice to the Cathedral, I looked elsewhere for a subject for my note-book, and found it in the picturesque tower of the Church of San Lorenzo, given by my eighty-eighth sketch.

The legend runs that this Church, and that of San Juan, were originally mosques; and that after the taking of the city from the Moors in 1149, they were applied to Christian uses. I am inclined to think this probable, although the detail is not anywhere Mahommedan, so far as the darkness of the interior would allow me to form any opinion. The great thickness of the walls, the mode of lighting, the form and proportions of the entrance archways (shown in my sketch) and the materials and mode of building of the base of the tower all seem to favour the supposition of an original Moorish construction. The octagonal form of tower is a favourite feature of this district, and occurs on a grand scale in the old Cathedral. The upper portion, at least, of this tower of San Lorenzo, may probably date from early in the fifteenth century.

PLATE 89

BARCELONA

OLD HOUSE CALLE DE SANTA LUCIA

PLATE † LXXXIX.

BARCELONA.

OLD HOUSE IN THE CALLE DE SANTA LUCIA.

AS Prescott[*] observes, "The City of Barcelona, which originally
gave its name to the county of which it was the capital, was
distinguished from a very early period by ample municipal privileges.
After the union with Arragon in the twelfth century, the monarchs of
the latter kingdom extended towards it the same liberal legislation; so
that by the thirteenth, Barcelona had reached a degree of commercial
prosperity rivalling that of any of the Italian Republics. She divided
with them the lucrative commerce with Alexandria; and her port
thronged with foreigners from every nation, became a principal
emporium in the Mediterranean for the spices, drugs, perfumes, and
other rich commodities of the East, whence they were diffused over
the interior of Spain and the European Continent."

Amongst its other merits was that of having established in 1401 the
first bank of Exchange and deposit in Europe—as well as of having
compiled the first written code amongst the Moderns of Maritime law.
Her great merchants were "magnificos" ennobled, not degraded as in
Castile, by connection with trade.

[*] "History of the Reign of Ferdinand and Isabella the Catholic." New York. 1845.
Page cxi.

The long civil war which began in 1462 and ended with the
surrender of the city to King Juan in 1472 was the first great check
the city received in its splendid career of prosperity.

The house I have sketched was doubtless well adapted to such
troublous times, affording comparative safety on its lower floors and
comparative air and comfort as its occupants mounted higher and higher.
It was probably built shortly after the middle of the fifteenth century,
revealing here and there traces of a French mason's handicraft. It
follows the type, not of the merchant's, but of the cavalier's house.
Such towers, half residence, half fortress, were, especially in the
south of Europe, far more numerous than one may now be justified in
supposing; and the more frequently Italian street views in pictures
and illuminated manuscripts are studied, the more natural and usual
appears what we now fancy to be strange and rare. With the
introduction of Renaissance architecture, the character of these quasi-
mediæval structures changed altogether.

Navagiero* writing of the condition of Barcelona in 1524, says that
" the houses are good and commodious, built of stone and not of earth,
as are those of the rest of Catalogna. Although lying on the sea it has
no port, but an arsenal, in which many galleys were wont to be
constructed, now there are none. Bread and wine are scarce, but of
every kind of fruit there is abundance. The cause is said to be that the
land is stripped of men through the war with King John on account
of his son Don Carlos."

Depopulated the city may have been, and its commerce may no
doubt have suffered in consequence, but the Catalonian character was
energetic and the city still preserved much of its previously accumulated

* 'Navagiero I. Viaggio fatto in Spagna.' Venice. 1563. Page 5.

wealth.   Merchants too have a knack of prospering in troublous times, especially those who thrive on profits upon imports.   Hence we still find merchant's houses of great comfort, although evidently constructed during the evil days of Barcelona.   Of one of these I furnish a good example, offering an interesting theme for comparison with the sketch now given, in my ninety-sixth sketch.

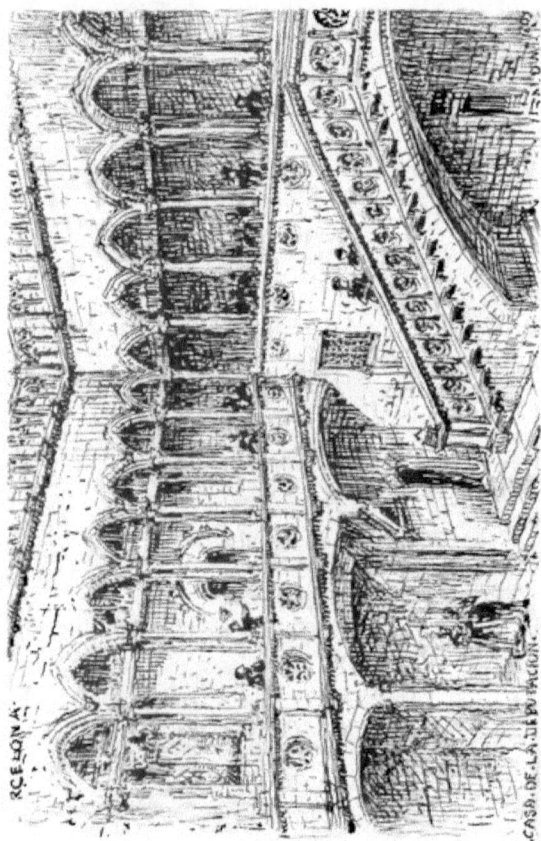

RCELONA

CASA DE LA DIPUTACIÓN

PLATE XC.

BARCELONA.

PATIO OF THE CASA DE LA DIPUTACION.

WITHIN the ancient " Palacio de la Diputacion " is preserved the elaborate late Gothic Chapel of St. George (protector of Catalonia) with a small but highly wrought entrance from the arcading on the first floor of the Patio de la Audiencia, represented in my sketch. This Patio is so called because its arcades, in which habitually sit many lawyers, and saunter many clients, lead to the Courts of Justice, in which causes are tried. The existence of this Chapel has, for ages, given a sort of prescriptive right to the public to invade the Patio, the Chapel, and its precincts, upon St. George's day. Of the gay scene which then takes place Parcerisa* has given an animated lithograph, showing the very different aspect it then wears to any it habitually presents.

Under any circumstances, however, its architecture, which is bold, even to the verge of rashness, gives it a permanent interest. It is a subject for wonder, that any structure in which the main supports of a heavy third story appear so insignificant as do the little marble columns

---

* " Recuerdos y Bellezas de España," por F. J. Parcerisa escrita y documentada, por P. Piferrer y J. Pi y Margall. Cataluña. Tome II., page 222.

(about two inches in diameter only) of the first floor of this Patio should have existed from mediæval days to our times. The truth, no doubt, is that the main weight of the walls of the top story, and of the roof, are carried by means of massive beams, acting as cantilevers, back to the walls which form the internal faces of the arcades, a device not quite maintaining that beautiful "lamp of truth" we are taught to look for in all mediæval designs. The users of the arcades have lately procured the building up of many of the arches, leaving windows to light the arcades. I have taken the liberty of omitting all of these but one, as I was desirous of showing, not what the lawyers have done, but what the original architects devised, no doubt as a "tour de force."

I was told upon the spot that this building up of the arches, the supports of which certainly appeared to my eye far too fragile for beauty, was a matter not of choice but of necessity.

BARCELONA
CASA DE LA DEPUTACIO

PLATE XCI.

BARCELONA.

DETAIL FROM THE CASA DE LA DIPUTACION.

IF Catalonian architecture differs from ordinary Spanish, and it is quite manifest from my sketch that it does in detail, as I have already shown that it does in system, the character of the Catalonian men and women differs even more markedly from that of the Spanish. While one of the latter in his laziness, as Marcos Obregon says, "ni come con gusto, ni duerme con quietud, ni descansa con reposo," the former, on the contrary, eat with appetite, sleep with tranquillity, and throw off their cares healthily in rest. The latter, in fact, chew but scarcely digest the bread of idleness, while the former thrive on that of industry. As a natural consequence, there is no love lost between the two races. The Castilian regards as mean and debasing the cultivation of the very mechanical arts, excellence in which the Catalonian well knows to be the source, not only of wealth, but of power and honour as well. To Barcelona belongs the credit of having been one of the first cities in the world, out of France, to establish gratuitous schools of design in which poor youths were taught specially to design for manufactures. Both

* " Travels through Spain and Part of Portugal." Sherwood Collection. London, 1818, page 281.

Laborde and Whittaker* testify to the extent and excellence of these schools at the end of the last century and beginning of the present. The latter, writing in 1803, says, "we visited the Academy of Arts instituted in the Palace of Commerce, and supported in the most magnificent manner by the merchants of Barcelona. We were conducted through a long suite of apartments, in which seven hundred boys were employed in copying and designing ; some of them, who display superior talents, are sent to Rome, and to the Academy of St. Fernando at Madrid; the others are employed in different ways by the merchants and manufacturers. The rooms are large and commodious, and are furnished with casts of celebrated statues and every proper apparatus. We observed a few drawings of considerable merit, produced by the scholars ; but the grand picture before us of liberality and industry, amply rewarded our visit ; and was the more striking to us, for having of late been continually accustomed to lament the traces of neglect and decay, so visibly impressed on every similar institution in the impoverished cities of Italy."

BARCELONA

PLATE XCII.

BARCELONA.

WINDOW FROM THE CASA DE LA DIPUTACION.

THIS quaint and very late specimen of Gothic, although Ecclesiastical enough in its sculpture, is purely domestic in its
architecture. The latter is in its character rather French or Burgundian
than Spanish, while the former was, I have little doubt, the work of a
native of the Peninsula. So far as I could see no preparation had ever
been made for glazing this window, and the wooden shutters, both in
their form and mode of joinery, were rather Moorish than Spanish.
No one can be surprised at such symptoms of internationality, in works
executed at a sea-port like Barcelona—in which the Arts, like the
prevalent language may have had a " lingua franca " of cosmopolitan
freedom from prejudice. In all such Gothic work, and indeed
in all building in Spain, however fantastic and not unfrequently over
intricate the detail may be, we scarcely ever observe any flimsiness, or
want of due substance in the constructional parts of any building. In
this matter the Spanish architects merit for attention to the erection of
permanent structures in all their styles the praise bestowed by Mr.
Street upon those mainly who wrought in the mediæval ones. Of those
last, the Spanish critics, who have been sometimes accused of overduly

estimating what they call Greco-Roman architecture, early showed what I regard as a fair appreciation. Antonio Ponz, for instance, in the last century certainly praised Berruguete, Covarrubias, and even Herrera in very glowing terms, but I know few writers who have better expressed an opinion as to the fitness of the mediæval styles, and especially the old Spanish system of the sturdiest construction, for ecclesiastical purposes.

Of this " Arquitectura Gótica," he says,* " nadie puede con razon decir, que falta en la majestad y el decoro : al contrario parece inventada para dárselo á los Templos, y casas del Señor. Los mas insignes Arquitectos han confessado su solidez, y han tenido mucho que admirar en el capricho de sus adornos, y en la prolixidad con que están acabadas todas sus partes. Muchos paises de Europa se precian de sus monumentos, y en España los hay magnificos, como son la Catedral de Burgos, la de Sevilla, Valencia, y otras."

* Ponz, Antonio, "Viage de España." Third Edition. Madrid. 1787. Vol. I. page 54.

BARCELONA

THE·TOWN·HALL·

PLATE XCIII.

BARCELONA.

DOORWAY IN THE TOWN HALL.

THE mission to Spain of the Count de Laborde on the part of the French Government at the moment when Napoleon I. thought he had the whole country within his grasp, was essentially economic in its object. Hence his accounts of, and investigations into, its past, present and future capabilities for trade are of far greater value than his topographical and archæological investigations, most of which are founded on the writings of Ponz and other well known authorities. While Spain was at the height of its prosperity, Seville and subsequently Cadiz commanded the South American trade, but Barcelona remained as it had been from a very early date, the great maritime means of communication and interchange of commodities between Spain and the rest of Europe. The business transactions carried on at its Lonja, or Bourse, and its Town Hall were very extensive, and these buildings were of commensurate importance. Our present sketch represents an internal doorway of the last named building, and the cosmopolitan character of its architecture, of probably

the commencement of the sixteenth century, will be manifest at a
glance. The following is Laborde's* epitome of the history of that
great foreign trade of which Barcelona once shared with Valencia and
Almeria almost a complete monopoly.

"The state of Spanish manufactures, in the fifteenth and sixteenth
century, will form a tolerably accurate clue to that of commerce at the
same period. The latter was then in a most flourishing condition, and
its ramifications extended to all parts of Europe. The cities of Medina
del Campo, Rio Seco, Burgos, Segovia, Toledo, Cuenca, Granada,
Almeria, Cordova, Jaen, Seville, Barcelona, Valencia, Ciudad Real,
and Sant' Jago, carried on a very extensive commerce. Almeria,
Valencia and Barcelona pushed their commercial concerns into Syria,
Egypt, Barbary, and the Archipelago. These cities were equally
important, in a mercantile view, with the Hanseatic towns. Barcelona
had a very great foreign trade; after the commencement of the
fourteenth century; under the Kings of Aragon it equipped and
maintained armed ships for the defence of the Catalonian coast and
the protection of its trade. It established factories in the extreme parts
of Europe and Asia, as far as the river Tanais; kept a consul, who
represented the city, and who was presented to Tamerlane the Great
in the year 1397, when he returned in triumph from his military
expedition into Muscovy and the Kipzac, a country lying east and west
of the Caspian Sea and the river Volga.

"Spain at that period had a large navy, and its shipping trade
was immense. If the account of Thome Cano in his 'Arte de
construir Naves' be admitted, it possessed a thousand merchant vessels

---

* "A View of Spain." Translated from the French of Alexander de Laborde. London.
1809. Vol. IV., pp. 372-3.

at a time when the European marine was far less extensive than it is at present."

To return for a moment to the picturesque doorway I have sketched. Its sculpture, which in execution is very good of its kind, is as completely Renaissance in character as its architecture is still Gothic ; it in fact corresponds exactly to Mudejar work, with this difference, that the admixture with the Gothic in this case is Plateresque, while in the Mudejar work it is Moorish.

BARCELONA·
·KNOCKER·TO·OLD·HOUSE·
·CALLE·SANTA·LUCIA·

·M.B.W.f 1869·

PLATE XCIV.

BARCELONA.

KNOCKER OF AN OLD HOUSE IN THE CALLE SANTA LUCIA.

IN the vicinity of the old church of Sta. Lucia yet exist at Barcelona several interesting stone houses of the fifteenth century. Upon the doors of these are to be still found specimens of excellent iron work of the same period. It is not however to be supposed that the Barcelonese possessed any very special gifts in this line, since evidences of almost equal dexterity are to be found scattered over the whole extent of the Peninsula. In the north and south alike, the " Rejas," or vast screens, sometimes of iron only, sometimes of brass and bronze, and sometimes of mixed metals, are yet to be found of great importance and interest. The most famous of the " Rejeros," as they were called, or makers of Rejas, were Francesco de Salamanca who flourished in 1533; Christobal Andino of 1540; Francesco de Vilalpando of 1561 : and Juan Bautista Celma of 1600. Because these men's names have become " household words" amongst all students of Spanish Art, it should not be forgotten that great men " to fortune and to fame unknown " lived before those whose good deeds and works encountered fitting record. By some of these were executed many of the various admirable specimens of metal work commented upon in terms of high praise by Ford, Street, O'Shea and other writers. The finest metal worker who really startled his contemporaries by the beauty and splendour of his workmanship, its "elaboracion y prolixedad," was the celebrated Henrique de Arfe, gold and silversmith of Leon, founder of a family which for several generations supplied artist-workmen in the precious metals whose fame rests upon the same platform as that of Cellini and Caradosso di Milano. His principal works were, according to the account given to us of them by his grandson Juan, in the "Varia Commensuracion," the custodias (or "ciboria" for holding the sanctified wafer) of the Cathedrals of Leon, Cordova, Toledo, and Sahagun. Of crosses, paxes, censers, pixes, feretories, candelabra, monstrances, lamps, &c., he scattered specimens broadcast throughout Spain. In all of them he showed, as his descendant declared, "El valor de su ingenio raro, con mayor efecto que puede escribirse."

As the present is the last occasion on which, in this volume at least, I may have to speak of mediæval metal work, and especially iron work, I may be allowed to allude very briefly to the two principal tools by which it was worked, viz.: the hammer and the pliers. In England and in France the first was used in preference at least to the last; while in Germany, Burgundy and the Low Countries, the last, was specially affected, and by its means foliage, both natural and conventional, was rendered with great skill, facility and taste. The Spaniards, as is proved by the present sketch, and that which follows it, were at an early period dexterous in the use of both tools: uniting the massive style engendered by the predominant use of the hammer with the more florid and fanciful manner springing out of the light and convoluted forms created by a more liberal use of the pliers.

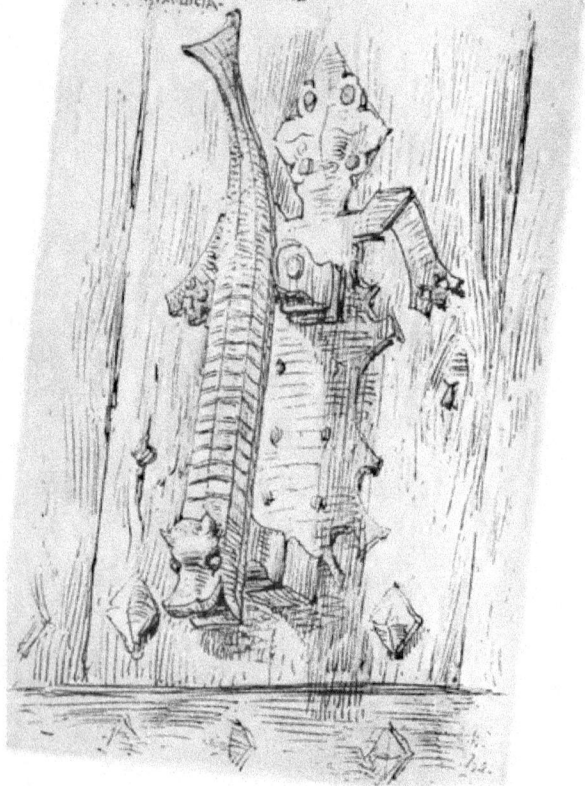

BARCELONA
KNOCKER TOOL HOUSE N 17 E
CALLE SANTA LUCIA

PLATE XCV.

BARCELONA.

KNOCKER TO AN OLD HOUSE IN THE CALLE SANTA LUCIA.

IN this fanciful little object we meet with another illustration of the spirit of humour as well as of dexterity in his craft, manifested in abundance by the excellent old ironworkers of Spain. Still good as the blacksmiths unquestionably were, the triumphs of Spanish metal working were chiefly embodied in the precious metals. It is rather in the cabinets of connoisseurs than in the churches of the country that specimens should be sought for to justify the splendid reputation those artist-workmen enjoyed in the palmy days of the Spanish Court and Church. Everywhere the traveller comes only now upon exhausted treasuries and emptied sacristies. Even since the days of Ford's inimitable handbook the spoiler has been rampant, and of the custodias and virils, the "blandones" and "portapaces" in which he delighted, so far as my perquisitions extended, scarcely a vestige was to be met with. Even since my sketches were made, the contents of the treasury of "Nuestra Señora del Pilar" have been brought to the hammer; and the pressure of other engagements alone prevented my return to Saragossa empowered to secure a share of those artistic curiosities for our National collection.

No doubt many beautiful specimens of Gothic precious metal work once adorned the principal mediæval ecclesiastical structures of Spain, but it was not till a later date that the most important and famous works, other than those already noticed (by Henrique de Arfe,) were produced. A brief notice of some of these from the pen of a cotemporary may not be altogether uninteresting.

"Although Renaissance architecture was introduced in Spain in a fully developed form before the middle of the sixteenth century, it was never thoroughly understood and adopted, we are told by Juan de Arphe y Villafañe,* in ecclesiastical plate, "until my father, Antonio de Arfe, began to use it in the Custodia of Santiago in Galicia and in that of Medina de Rioseco, and in the portable shrine of Leon."

"In all his work he evidenced an imperfect knowledge of good style, introducing fanciful columns of irregular proportions according to his own fancy. Juan Alvarez, who was a native of Salamanca, died in the prime of his life in the service of Don Carlos of Austria. For this reason he left no evidence of his rare talent in any public performance. Alonso Beceril obtained reputation in his turn on account of having made in his studio the Custodia of Cuenca. This work secured the approbation of every artist in Spain who at that time was really learned in Art. Juan de Orna was an excellent plate-worker in Burgos. Juan Ruiz,† a disciple of my grandfather, made the Custodias of Jaen, Baza, and that of San Pablo of Seville. He was the

---

* Even better known as "El Vandolino."

† "Varia Commensuracion para la escultura y Arquitectura, sexta impresion." Madrid, 1773. p. 222.

first who used the lathe for forming plate in Spain; he set the fashion for the principal pieces of silver services for the table, and instructed workmen throughout Andalusia. All the above artists, and others, began to give elegant shapes to the principal objects made in silver and gold for the use of the church, each one improving in symmetry and general excellence upon the works of his predecessors until those types became established which I am now about to describe."

Juan de Arphe proceeds, after complimenting Philip II. on his majestic works at the Escorial, to give the forms and proportions of the five orders, and their application to every variety of silversmith's work, recognised as suitable for employment in sacred offices and ecclesiastical rites and ceremonies in his time.

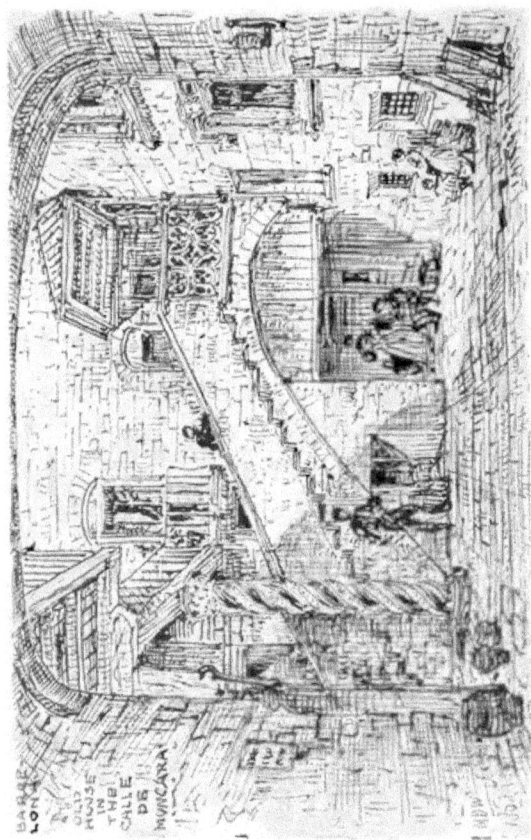

BARBE LONGA

AN OLD HOUSE IN THE CALLE DE MURCARA

PLATE XCVI.

—

BARCELONA.

COURTYARD OF AN OLD HOUSE IN THE CALLE DE MONCARA.

IN noticing my ninety-first sketch I took occasion to comment on the difference which obtained between Spanish and Catalonian architecture, and Spanish and Catalonian character. Both are pressed upon one's attention in looking over a house which, like the one I have sketched in the Calle de Moncara at Barcelona, appears to have been the comfortable home of a well-to-do merchant, with roomy stores and warehouses on the ground floor facing the entrance, domestic offices to the left, and counting-house and living rooms on the first floor, with bedrooms above. As is becoming in the house of one welcoming alike buyer and seller, we find a total absence of that almost Asiatic privacy which the Spaniards generally, and especially the Andalusians, appear in their homes to have adopted from Moorish models. Under the old Counts of Barcelona the architecture of the city had no doubt been mainly French. After the annexation of the city to the crown of Aragon, the architecture became tinctured with detail corresponding with much yet to be seen at Saragossa and elsewhere in Aragon, and finally after the consolidation of the whole monarchy by the marriage of Ferdinand and Isabella, and the expulsion of the Moors, Barcelonese architecture fell under the Plateresque revival and the subsequent Greco-Roman mania which affected all Spain. The date of erection of the house of which I now give a sketch, appears to have brought it under the second of these two sets of conditions. In the twisted column, its cap and base, and some other features, we may recognise the Aragonese style, while in the staircase and some of the windows there is to be traced, I consider, a decided French influence.

In spite of legislative assimilation, the Catalonians have never been able to cordially adopt a Spanish nationality. They have never warmly responded to the caresses of their monarchs. Even as late as 1802, when Charles IV. paid a visit to Barcelona with the infamous Godoy, and a retinue like an army, and drew some eighty thousand strangers the city, a visitor in the following year records that "the Catalans felt a generous pride in observing that no accident or quarrel occurred on that occasion, and no life was lost, *notwithstanding the enmity subsisting between them and the Spaniards.*"[*] Whittaker further illustrates this mutual jealousy and spiteful feeling by the following characteristic anecdote :—"This enmity," he says, "is carried to such a height that when it was proposed to strike a medal in honour of the King's visit, the Academy of Arts of St. Fernando, at Madrid, were requested to superintend the execution; but this body, actuated by a most illiberal and unworthy spirit, endeavoured to excuse themselves, and made every possible delay, which so enraged the Catalans, that they withdrew the business from their hands, and trusted it to their own academy. The medal was produced in a month, and remains a record rather of their loyal zeal, than of their ability in the fine arts."

* "Travels through Spain and Part of Portugal," by the Rev. G. D. Whittaker in 1803 Sherwood's Collection, London, 1813, page 279.

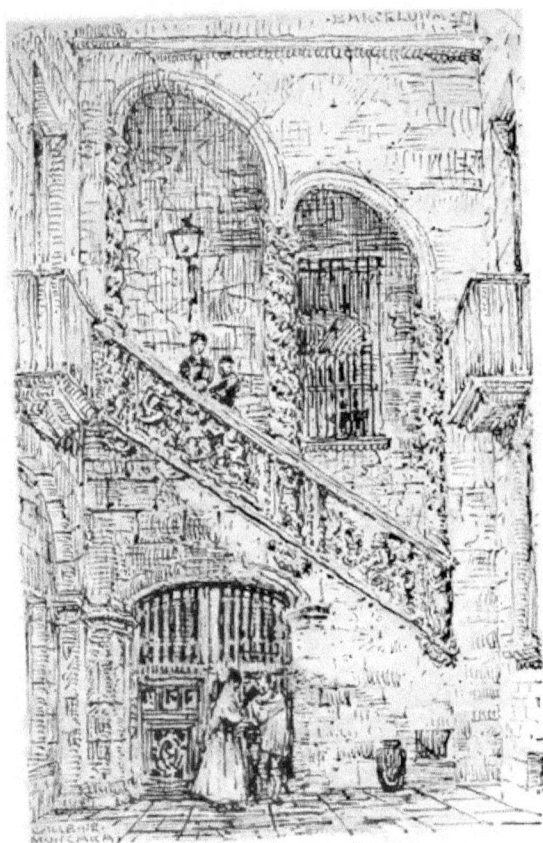

PLATE XCVII.

BARCELONA.

STAIRCASE OF AN OLD HOUSE IN THE CALLE DE MONGARA.

I AM induced to give this one little specimen of what the Spaniards call "Churriguerismo" for these reasons: 1stly, because it is a prettier example than usual of the style practised early in the eighteenth century by the fashionable José Churriguerra—the William Kent of Spanish architecture; 2ndly, because it afforded a good specimen of the comfortable house of a rich Barcelonese merchant of the last century; and 3rdly, on account of the singular arrangement of the jointing of the masonry, which converts the apparently double arch into very little else than one tolerably stable spanning of the whole space.

In describing my eighty-fifth sketch I alluded to the fact that the trade of Spain gradually fell into the hands mainly of foreigners, and especially at first of the Genoese, the difference between them and the native Spanish merchant being that while the former were crafty, industrious and dishonest, the latter were stupid and lazy, but (except in the matter of smuggling) strictly honest. Plenty of witness is borne by different writers to both facts. Quevedo, for instance,

abounds in hits at the Genoese and other Italians. "Give an Italian
to the Devil," he says in his "El Alguazil Endemoniado," "and the
old gentleman won't try to take him, for an Italian would take away
the Devil himself."[*] Elsewhere in the same satire he cautions his
readers telling them that they are bound to know "that in Spain
the mysteries of the accounts of the Genoese are disastrous for the
millions that come from the Indies, and that the cannons of their
pens are batteries for purses. There are no incomes which, if they
once get into the strokes of their pens, and the inkholders of their
inkstands, escape without drowning."[†]

The poco-curante honesty of the Spaniard on the other hand,
the "poco-curanteeism" at least an inheritance from the East, kept
business in his hands which, but for his reliability, ought according
to every recognised law of probability in trade, to have left him
before it did. Laborde, a writer by no means inclined to take
too favourable a view of the national character, confesses that
"Spanish probity is proverbial, and it conspicuously shines in
commercial relations. Good faith and punctuality are generally
prevalent among merchants, the instances of deception, negligence,
fraudulent dealing and non-fulfilment of engagements, so generally
in the trading world, being unknown to and not practised amongst

---

[*] "Days al Diablo un Italiano, y no le torna el Diablo, por que ay Italiano que tomara al Diablo."

[†] "Y haveys de saber que en España los misterios de las cuentas de los Ginoveses, son dolorosos para los cudares que vienen de las Indias, y que los cañones de sus plumas son de bateria contra las bolsas, y no ay renta que si la cogen en medio el tajo de sus plumas, y el jarama de su tinta no la ahoguen." (The reader will observe the double meaning which points Quevedo's sarcasm—"cañones" express at the same time quills and cannons.)—"Sueños Discursos por Don Francisco de Quevedo Villegas Zaragoza." 1627. Page 19.

them." As an illustration, Laborde mentions some coined silver sent home in the year 1654, which was paid away by the Spanish merchants, and was subsequently discovered to have been debased. Not only were the Spanish merchants eager to make good the loss to those who had dealt with them, but having discovered the culprit they obtained his conviction, and the wretched man was publicly burnt alive. In spite of honesty, however, trade and commerce will not thrive in any country in which they are looked upon as degrading. Catalonia might work, since he was but half a Spaniard. Spain proper, however, was quite willing to pay any one who would work for him, and as with his increase of wealth his wants became more and more artificial and luxurious, the swarms of foreigners he harboured about him to do his bidding, increased to an unprecedented extent. The Countess D'Aulnois gives a capital account of the state of things in this respect in her time (circâ 1679).

"Spain," she says,* "cannot well be without commerce with France, not only on the frontiers of Biscai and Arragon, where it hath been almost ever permitted, but through the whole country where it is prohibited, for Provence hath ever had correspondencies in the kingdom of Valentia, by its necessity of the others commodities ; and for the same reason Britaign, Normandy, and other parts on the ocean have continually sent theirs to Cadiz and Bilbo. I speak not of corn and stuffs of all sorts brought from that country, but even of ironwork and swords ; by which it appears a mistake to think that in these dayes the best come of Spain. No more being now made at Toledo, few but forrain are used, unless a very small quantity that come from Biscai, which are excessively dear.

* " Letter of a Lady's Travels into Spain." London. Ninth Edition.

C /

"It is, moreover, hard to imagine how much Spain suffers for want of manufactures. So few artificers remain in its towns, that native commodities are carried abroad to be wrought in forrain countries. Wools and silks are transported raw, and being spun and weaved in England, France, and Holland, return thither at dear rates. The land itself is not tilled by the people it feeds. In seed time, harvest, and vintage, husbandmen come from Bearn and other parts of France, who get a great deal of money by sowing and reaping their corn, and dressing and cutting their vines. Carpenters and masons are (for the most part) also strangers, who will be paid treble what they can get in their own country. In Madrid there is hardly a waterbearer that is not a foreigner, such are also the greatest part of shoomakers and taylors, and it is believed the third of these come only to get a little money and afterwards return home; but none thrive so much as architects, masons, and carpenters. Almost every house hath wooden windows (here being no glass), and a balcony jutting into the street.

GERONA·
OLD·HOUSE·NEAR·THE·
ESTRELLA·DE·ORO·

PLATE XÖVIII.

GERONA.

OLD HOUSE NEAR THE ESTRELLA DE ORO.

I F my last sketch illustrated the regular rich merchant's house of the eighteenth century—symbol of peace and plenty, police and protection, the kind of residence I now submit to the reader's attention is cast in quite a different key. It is essentially a fighter's house, the only kind of structure in which (before the use of gunpowder) a family could hold its own for months of foreign siege or protracted street fighting. Gerona has always been, as we shall have occasion to recognize in examining its fine old walls, almost a frontier city, struggled for repeatedly by Christian and by Moor. The house I have sketched is one of the earliest and most complete of its class I have ever seen, the lower half alone having been materially altered from its original construction. It dates in all probability from the middle of the twelfth century, and yet stands strong and stalwart in a quarter of the city in which very little of anything not comparatively of yesterday meets the wandering visitor's eye. On comparing this sketch with that from a house at Barcelona (No. 96) erected at least three hundred years later, it will be found that the type furnished by the earliest in date had changed but little in the interval. Hence we may fairly infer that the conditions of insecurity affecting domestic life had scarcely varied in Catalonia during the whole of that term. In fact, it was not until the invention of printing spread abroad the elements of education, and brought about changes in social systems, that men began to dream of peace and security ensured by other preservatives from danger than heavy armour and fortress-like houses.

GERONA.
UPPER PART OF OLD HOUSE
NEAR SAINT-FELIX

PLATE XϕIX.

c/

GERONA.

UPPER PART OF OLD HOUSE AND SPIRE OF THE CHURCH OF SAINT "FELIU."

THE west front of the Cathedral at Gerona stands at the top of a noble flight of eighty-six steps, and these ascended, platforms are reached on the west and south of the splendid pile from which fine views over the city and its environs are obtained. The sketch now under notice was taken from the southern platform, the wall enclosing which upon the west cuts off something like thirty feet in height of the fine old house which forms the principal object in the sketch. Its uppermost story, with its continuous arcade, has a symmetrical and agreeable effect, and appears to have been the only portion of the building really suitable for habitation according to modern views as to the value of abundant light and air. On the right is seen the cathedral well, the waters of which have no doubt alike served for the bodily and spiritual ablutions of Mahommedan and Christian, since cathedral, mosque, and then again cathedral, have existed in turn upon the same site from the days of Charlemagne to the present time. During the Moorish occupation in the eighth century the Christians were permitted to worship in the original church of San Feliu (Felix) the truncated spire of the successor to which appears in my sketch between the old house, and the south-west angle of the cathedral, shown on the extreme right. The present church, dedicated to San Feliu, dates probably from the early part of the fourteenth century. Its history has been clearly traced by Mr. Street from a comparison of the building with the particulars given and documents quoted in the "España Sagrada." "The steeple is said to have been finished in 1392. Pedro Zacoma having acted as architect as late as A.D. 1376." It was struck by lightning in the year 1581, and has remained ever since shorn of its fair proportions, as we now see it.

San Feliu, as he is popularly called, was an early Spanish Christian, deacon to San Narciso, the Martyr, Protector and "Generalissimo" of the See of Gerona.

GERONA · OLD WALLS · NEAR · SAN · PEDRO ·

PLATE φ.   c/

GERONA.

OLD WALLS NEAR THE MONASTERY OF SAN PEDRO.

FROM the date at least on which Charlemagne captured Gerona from the Moors, it has been an essentially fighting city; manned through all history, and under every circumstance of siege and occupation, by men and women of the sternest courage and determination it has been held with the utmost tenacity, as really even more than Figueras (the actual frontier town), the key to the easiest line of advance from France into Spain. Hence the strength and interest of its fine old walls, which in spite of every ancient and modern vicissitude, still retain more curious features of middle age defence than, to the best of my belief, any other city of Spain, with the exception of Avila. As will be seen from my sketch, the apse of the fine old Romanesque church of San Pedro, which actually forms a bulwark, has been raised so as to bring it into practical fighting order, and the covered galleries for marksmen, with bow and cross bow, matchlock and firelock, still extend from it to the north and to the south in easily to be recognised, and still fairly complete, galleries of well-sheltered communication. The present aspect of the north of Gerona forms a fair pendant to the description Charles Didier gives of

its sister fortress to the side of France, Figueras. He says, "Tout a
un air d'abandon et de désolation les casernes sont magnifiques, mais
désertes ; les casemates spacieuses, mais vides ; les longues herbes de
la solitude croissent partout, et la seule partie des bâtiments qui soit
aujourd'hui de première nécessité, l'infirmerie, n'est point terminée ;
les pierres à moitié taillées jonchent le sol et sont couvertes de mousse.
J'errai longtemps seul dans ce silencieux désert sans rencontrer personne ;
de loin en loin seulement, j'apercevais quelque sentinelle perdue à
la pointe d'une demi-lune et nonchalamment appuyée contre les
canons et les mortiers ; de gros rats rongeaient en paix les affuts ; ils
se sont si bien emparés du lieu, que mon approche les dérangeait à
peine ; je n'avais pas fait trois pas, qu'ils se remettaient à l'œuvre.
Voilà sous quels traits l'Espagne apparaît au voyageur qui vient de
France, triste et frappante image d'une chute sans exemple et d'une
misère sans terme."*

One would have preferred receiving from any other than a
Frenchman so dreary a picture of the desolation mainly wrought by
Frenchmen.   Returning to Gerona, to which Didier's description
applies (as I have already stated) nearly as well as to Figueras, in sight
of which he may have written it, we shall find Mr. Street no less
strongly impressed than I was with what Spain owes to France in the
matter. "All this havoc and ruin is owing," he says, "like so much
that one sees in Spain, to the action of the French troops during the
Peninsular War." It is however but just to the French to add that the
Spaniards are not like them, endowed with wonderful recuperative
energy.

* "Une Année en Espagne," par Charles Didier, 1837.

www.ingramcontent.com/pod-product-compliance
Lightning Source LLC
Chambersburg PA
CBHW031824270326
41932CB00008B/541